Day bomber underwing marking style to August 1934

Day bomber underwing marking style from August 1934

Night bomber underwing marking style to August 1934

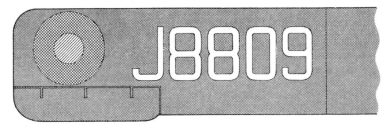

Night bomber underwing marking style from August 1934

Colour key

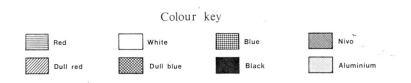

Red   White   Blue   Nivo

Dull red   Dull blue   Black   Aluminium

bombing colours

bombing colours

British bomber camouflage and markings 1914-1937

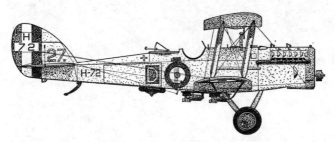

BRUCE ROBERTSON

Patrick Stephens
London

ISBN 0 85059 093 0
First edition—August 1972

Text set in 9 on 10pt Times Roman type.
Printed in Great Britain
for Patrick Stephens Ltd, 9 Ely Place, London EC1N 6SQ
by Blackfriars Press Ltd, Leicester and
bound by Hunter & Foulis Ltd, Edinburgh.

introduction

BOMBING COLOURS first appeared as a series of articles by Bruce Robertson in *Airfix Magazine,* and has been put into book form as a companion volume to *Fighting Colours* by Michael J. F. Bowyer which is still in print. Extra text, drawings and photographs have been added to *Bombing Colours* to enlarge the coverage of bomber markings in the First World War and the years of uneasy peace that followed. A further book, by Michael J. F. Bowyer, is planned to continue the bomber marking story from 1937, throughout the Second World War and its aftermath, up to the present day.

The reason for the 'split' at 1937 is conditioned solely by the subject matter; that year saw the close of an era in British service aircraft markings and the start of a new. The shades of war, it could be said, were evinced literally by the changes in RAF aircraft colours in 1937.

The dual authorship of Michael J. F. Bowyer and Bruce Robertson is not a case of two writers being commissioned independently, for they have worked together on publishing ventures for 20 years. Continuity of presentation is maintained by the services of expert artist Alfred M. Alderson.

The authors and publishers would like to thank the contributors of photographs and they are credited in the captions. They are also grateful to Jack Long, Les Rogers and all others who contributed reference material.

author's preface

BOMBING COLOURS 1914-1937 aims not only to show how British bombing aircraft of this period were marked, but also to explain the significance of these markings. By British bombers I mean bombing aircraft of the Royal Naval Air Service and Royal Flying Corps from 1914 to April 1918, when these two services merged to form the Royal Air Force which is then traced to 1937.

I have also included as bombers the early aircraft of 1914-16 whose duties, not clearly defined, included bombing. Fighter and training aircraft adapted for bombing are also featured. Aircraft that carried bombs, but whose primary task was general duties, such as the Westland Wapiti, army co-operation aircraft such as the Hawker Audax, or bomber seaplanes such as the Fairey IIIB, have not been covered since these may well appear in further books in the series, under titles defining other roles.

London, February 1972   **Bruce Robertson**

contents

illustrations

diagrams in text

Chapter 1

Bombers before fighters

MILITARY AIRCRAFT were developed for scouting, but when offensive action was first taken it was by bombing. Furthermore, it was carried out by aircraft designed for other purposes.

At the beginning of the First World War the British navy and army each had their separate air arms, the Royal Naval Air Service and the Royal Flying Corps respectively. The standard finish in both Services was plain doped white fabric and varnished wood, so that their colouring was 'natural'. Their only mandatory marking was a serial number and the two Services had agreed a common numbering system in November 1912 for all aircraft.

Aircraft were simply numbered from No 1, replacing earlier markings used by units which varied considerably. RNAS aircraft, belonging to the senior service, were allotted Nos 1 to 200 and the RFC No 201 upwards. However, by August 4 1914, the day the United Kingdom declared war on Germany, the Navy had taken up their first 1-200 allocation and had been allotted a further batch of numbers—801-1600, later they took up 3001-4000 and 8001-10000. The RFC used the intervening numbers and thus, for the period 1914-16 before prefix letters were introduced, it was possible to differentiate between aircraft of the RNAS and RFC by the blocks of numbers issued.

In 1914 the numbers were marked on the rudder as it was the only position which could be standardised. Maurice Farman pushers and Bleriot tractor monoplanes had no covered fuselage and therefore the rudder was the only covered vertical area. The RFC marked the numbers, in general, in black 18-inch digits, while the Navy, to give the numbers more emphasis, first painted a white patch on the off-white finish of the rudder fabric as a background for the number.

Undoubtedly the most famous bomber of 1914 was No 50 a BE2a used as the personal aircraft of Commander C. R. Samson. After being flown to Belgium in late August 1914, with other aircraft from Eastchurch, to form a nucleus of a naval wing guarding the Channel ports and to attack Zeppelin bases, it made its first bombing flight on September 14. On that occasion, Samson set out from Dunkerque (Dunkirk) at 08.50 hrs and made a 100-minute flight over Armentières, expending two bombs on a group of four cars with some 40 men around them.

When the RNAS launched an air attack from Antwerp on the Zeppelin sheds at Düsseldorf and Cologne on September 23, Major C. L. Gerrard, Royal Marine Light Infantry, set out on No 50, followed by No 149 Sopwith Churchill, No 169 Sopwith Tabloid and No 906, an impressed Sopwith Tractor Biplane. None of these aircraft bore any marking other than their black serial number on a white patch.

An epic attack by Sopwith Tabloid No 168—a type regarded later as an embryo fighter rather than a bomber—resulted in the Zeppelin Z.IX being blown up in its hangar at Düsseldorf on October 8.

Perhaps the most famous of all the early bombing raids was that by a batch of Avro 504s, straight from the factory, taken by ship and rail to Belfort to carry out an attack on the Friedrichshafen Zeppelin sheds on the banks of Lake Constance. Four Avros were sent—No 179, the naval prototype and Nos 873, 874 and 875, the first production for the RNAS. No 179 unfortunately broke a tailskid on take-off and was grounded, but the other three attacked, damaging a Zeppelin and destroying the associated gas works. No 873 was lost on the raid.

The first Avro 504s in naval service were known as Avro 179 Type after the serial number of the prototype—a case of a serial number conditioning the type name. The famous Short 184 seaplanes also derived their type number from the serial number of the prototype—184.

National markings introduced

In 1914 there was no internationally accepted ruling on marking aircraft with an indication of their nationality, although the French had led the way in 1912 with a representation of their Tricolour in the roundel form which they use to this day. The need for such markings by the British and German forces had not been foreseen, until the roar of musketry that greeted friend and foe alike in the air decided the issue that some indication was necessary.

The Germans used their Black Cross marking from as early as September 28 according to a report on that day by Lieutenant Osmond, RNAS, who made his observation from an armoured car. By that time several British pilots, having been fired upon by their own infantry, took the initiative and painted a Union Jack under the wings of their craft. This was also marked on the rudder, fin or fuselage sides, for in a forced landing British pilots were often treated with suspicion or hostility by the French who had no means of checking their identity. Thus, the first markings on British service aircraft, apart from serials, were to protect the crews from their friends !

The Admiralty on October 26 made Union Jack markings on the underside of wings compulsory for RNAS aircraft, but by that time the RFC had already found the marking impracticable. It is an indisputable fact that shape is more easily discerned at distance than colours, and the central Red Cross of St George, that forms the basis of the Union Flag, was the most prominent feature of the marking—and easily confused with the German Cross. The RNAS also came to realise this a little later and each service issued their separate instructions.

By the end of 1914 two different forms of national markings were in use. The General Headquarters of the RFC in the Field decreed a roundel form on December 11, based on the French roundel but with the order of the colours reversed; six days later the Admiralty issued instructions to mark a red ring with a white centre on the wings of all RNAS aircraft. For a time the Union Jack remained officially appropriate for fuselage sides and rudders, but some pilots marked the Union Jack under wings additional to roundels, lest the significance of the latter would not be appreciated.

Bombing aircraft of both services were probably the first to bear the new national marking forms. In the RFC the aircraft were predominantly reconnaissance aircraft, used for occasional bomb-dropping and the odd Tabloid was used for scouting, not fighting. In the RNAS bombing aircraft were undoubtedly the first to bear the new red ring marking. These were the Short Seaplanes taken in carriers of the Harwich Force to attack Cuxhaven; Nos 119 and 120 were on *Engadine*, Nos 135, 136 and 811 on *Riviera* and Nos 812, 814 and 815 on *Empress*. Para 11 of the operational orders issued by the Commodore of the Harwich Force as early as December 2 state: 'It is probable that our seaplanes will be attacked by hostile seaplanes. Aerial guns are to be manned, and the greatest care is to be taken that our seaplanes are not fired at by mistake. They can be distinguished by a large ring painted in red under each wing, and also Union Jacks'.

During 1915 the national markings on aircraft were further modified and then standardised. In May 1915 the RFC introduced rudder striping in national colours, with the blue leading from the rudder post, then white and red trailing. From this same time it was notified that Union Jacks on fins or fuselage sides were no longer appropriate. Next month the RFC made it mandatory for all aircraft with covered fuselages to have roundels on fuselage sides and wings. By late June the markings had been standardised throughout the aircraft of the RFC on the Western Front. The actual aircraft concerned are those shown tabulated by squadrons on page 22.

Presentation markings

Organisations in Britain and the Colonies early in the war launched a scheme to raise an Imperial Air Flotilla. For every £1500 donated a BE2c would be given a name decreed by the donor; for larger sums other aircraft types could be 'purchased'. In fact the money went to a central fund and a normal production aircraft bore the presentation details.

The Overseas Club were responsible for raising money for several hundred aircraft and these aircraft bore names of faraway places; eg, Overseas Club No 33, an RE7, bore the name THE AKYAB in No 19 Squadron with which it served before the squadron left for France. A similar fund was started in India; a resulting example in No 16 Squadron was BE2c, PUNJAB No 2. A fund started by a Mr Alma Baker in Malaya brought a good response to which a No 52 Squadron BE2c bore witness with the marking MALAYA XVI MENANG on the fuselage.

Squadron markings

Early in 1916 a need for the identification of particular squadron aircraft had arisen and some units had experimented with embellishing their aircraft, to the wrath of GHQ who banned all unofficial markings, but did

15

introduced a standard scheme, promulgated on April 23 1916. This consisted of simple devices and bars marked on the fuselage side. Initially only ten squadrons, all equipped with BE2cs, were concerned; these were Nos 2, 4, 5, 6, 7, 8, 10, 12, 15 and 16 Squadrons.

Figure 1: *The first squadron markings as introduced in April 1916.*

(Drawings continued on page 21.)

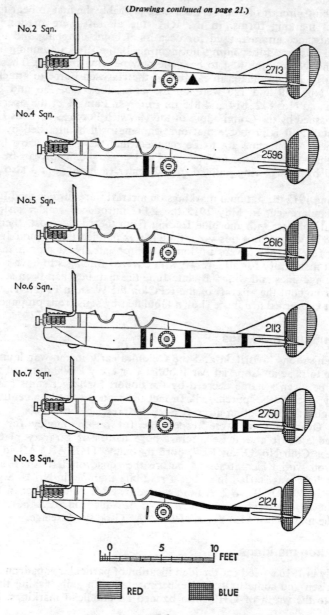

No.2 Sqn. — 2713

No.4 Sqn. — 2596

No.5 Sqn. — 2616

No.6 Sqn. — 2113

No.7 Sqn. — 2750

No.8 Sqn. — 2124

0   5   10 FEET

RED   BLUE

16

1 *The RE1 of 1913 when finishes were in general clear doped fabric, varnished plywood (fuselage top decking forward) and sheet metal (engine side cowling and tank)* (RAF 114).

2 *It takes an incident such as this to give a clear indication of upper- and lower-surface markings on early aircraft when flying photographs were rare. This view of a BE2, late in 1914, shows upper-surfaces unmarked in contrast to the under-surfaces shown in the view below of the same aircraft at the same time* (J. M. Bruce/G. S. Leslie Collection).

3 *National markings in 1914 were displayed for the benefit of those on the ground and were not always marked on fuselage sides, let alone upper-surfaces (see photo above)* (J. M. Bruce/G. S. Leslie Collection).

4 *A torpedo-bomber of 1914, the prototype Short 184 whose serial number conditioned the type number 184 for the most famous seaplane of the war* (J. M. Bruce/G. S. Leslie Collection).

5 *A Breguet bomber used by the RNAS with a 'double-Jack' rudder marking* (via E. F. Cheesman).

6 *When rudders were first striped, the RFC moved the serial number presentation from the rudder to the fin, but in the RNAS the serial number was then displayed on the fuselage, as shown on this BE2c* (Real Photographs).

7 *Serial of BE2c 2008 marked across rudder stripes (an exception in 1915, that became the rule later) and roundels marked on the tailplane, a practice that persisted in some squadrons until early 1917* (via Frank Yeoman).

8 *One of the anomalies when camouflage was introduced in 1916—an uncamouflaged BE12 with a camouflaged tail fin* (Real Photographs 1825).

18

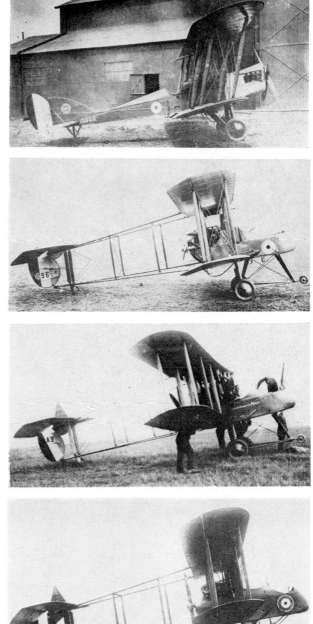

9 *No 10000, the only British military aircraft to have a five digit serial number. This BE2c for the RNAS bears its maker's trademark—Blackburn* (J. M. Bruce/ G. S. Leslie Collection).

10 *There were irregularities in the detail markings of FE2bs; compare this standard factory finish of a contract-built FE2b with the examples below* (Real Photographs 668).

11 *Royal Aircraft Factory-built FE2b A'9, with nacelle roundel deleted, rudder stripes marked obliquely and inscription—Presented by Residents of the PUNJAB* (Imperial War Museum Q27644).

12 *FE2d A'6389 as built by Boulton & Paul. The apostrophe in the serial is just visible on the rudder of this machine and in the photo above* (Real Photographs 664).

13 *On camouflaged surfaces in 1916-17 it was usual to mark roundels as large as the wing chord allowed, with a one-inch wide outline, as revealed by this FE* (Ministry of Defence).

14 *E7075, a late production FE2b in black night camouflage without roundels and rudder stripes* (Imperial War Museum).

15 *Factory finish of a late production DH4 showing areas of battleship grey (forward and rear fuselage), chocolate brown (mid-fuselage and wings) and clear doped fabric (wheel discs)* (RNZAF).

16 *Factory finish of a late production DH9 showing grey and brown areas for wood and fabric respectively similar to the DH4 above* (RNZAF).

20

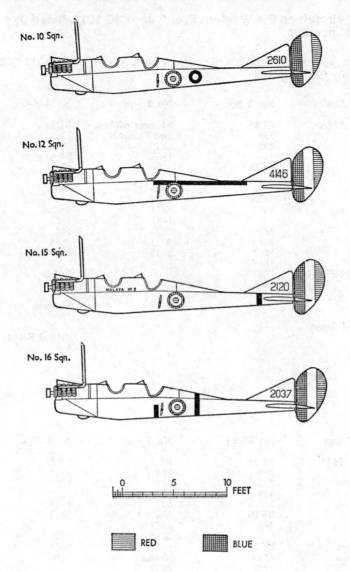

No. 10 Sqn.   2610

No. 12 Sqn.   4146

No. 15 Sqn.   MALAYA No 2   2120

No. 16 Sqn.   2037

0   5   10 FEET

▥ RED   ▦ BLUE

New trend

Until the end of 1916 bombing was mainly carried out by BE squadrons as a role additional to their normal spotting tasks. When replaced by RE8s in 1917 they concentrated more on their primary task and bombing became the work of specialist bombing squadrons.

Another new trend in 1916 was probably the greatest change in the character of British service aircraft ever to take place—the adoption of camouflage colours for aircraft throughout the two Services.

B   21

RFC aircraft on the Western Front, June 30 1915, listed by serial number

(These aircraft were predominantly reconnaissance aircraft, but with a capacity for bombing.)

No 1 Sqn	No 2 Sqn	No 3 Sqn	No 4 Sqn
Avro 504A	**BE2a**	**Morane Biplanes**	**BE2a**
752	336	**and Parasols**	234
758	492	1849	
769		1862	**BE2b**
773	**BE2b**	1866	493
2859	396	1870	705
4223		1873	796
	BE2c	1874	
Morane	1652	1875	**BE2c**
1885	1657	1881	1678
1896	1659	5021	1686
1897	1660	5023	1698
5006	1662	5033	1701
	1669		
Caudron	1687		**Voisin**
1884			5028
1885			
1891			**Morane**
			587
Bristol Scout			
1603			**Bristol Scout**
			648
Martinsyde			
748			

No 5 Sqn	No 6 Sqn	No 7 Sqn	No 8 Sqn
Avro 504A	**BE2a**	**RE5**	**BE2c**
637	206	617	1665
750	241	631	1702
755	468	674	1750
782		677	1783
783	**BE2b**	678	2030
4225	484	2457	
		2458	**BE8**
Vickers	**BE2c**		740
Gunbus	1680	**Voisin**	2130
1637	1781	1883	
1651		1898	**Bristol Scout**
2873	**Bristol Scout**	5001	1610
	1611	5014	1613
Bristol Scout		5025	
1603		5026	
Martinsyde		**Bristol Scout**	
2823		1606	

NB: Squadron Nos 9-15 had not yet arrived at the Front.

No 16 Sqn	In reserve	Under repair or reconstruction	
BE2c	**Caudron**	**Avro 504A**	**FE2b**
1676	5016	398	4292
1684	5020	2858	
1694	5031		**Martinsyde**
1699	5032	**BE2a**	2449
1752	5035	242	
1792	5038	314	**Maurice**
		385	**Farman**
Maurice	**Martinsyde**	666	1857
Farman	743		5036
5004		**BE2b**	
5009	**Maurice**	687	**Morane**
5015	**Farman**		1863
5019	1869	**BE2c**	1882
5027	1893	1656	5007
	5008	1658	
	5030	1668	**Vickers**
		1670	**Gunbus**
		1748	1616
		1753	1638
	Morane Voisin	1782	1650
	5034 1850	1784	
	1860		
	Vickers 1879		
	Gunbus 1890	**Bristol Scout**	
	1639 5017	1608	
	2872	1609	

RFC aircraft on the Western Front, August 31 1915, listed by serial number

(This list makes an interesting comparison with the previous one, which gives the position two months earlier, by showing the gradual attempt at type standardisation within each squadron and the large change in the aircraft held during those two months of continuous operations.)

No 1 Sqn	No 2 Sqn	No 3 Sqn	No 4 Sqn
Avro 504A	**BE2c**	**Morane**	**BE2a**
758	(Renault engine)	1849	368
769	1652	1863	
773	1657	1870	**BE2b**
4223	1659	1874	493
		1881	746
Morane	**BE2c**	5033	
1894	(RAF engine)	5034	**BE2c**
1897	1669	5039	(RAF engine)
5006	1687	5041	1658
5046	1703	5044	1678
5048	1710	5045	1701
5051	1716	5055	1726
5052	1729		1781
	1732		2001
Caudron	1734		2007
1884	2673		2035
1885			
			Morane
	Bristol Scout		587
	4667		
			Bristol Scout
			684

No 5 Sqn	No 6 Sqn	No 7 Sqn	No 8 Sqn
Avro 504A	**BE2a**	**RE5**	**BE2a**
783	206	617	336
784		2457	
785	**BE2c**	2458	**BE2c**
4225	(RAF engine)		(RAF engine)
	1680	**Voisin**	1704
Vickers	1706	5001	1709
Gunbus	1713	5025	1711
1651	1714	5028	1721
2874	1718		1723
2878	1740	**Bristol Scout**	1725
	2031	4668	2008
Bristol Scout	2674		2030
1603		**BE2c**	2039
	FE2a	(Renault engine)	
BE2c	2864	1788	
(RAF engine)	4227		
1728	4253	**BE2c**	
1736		(RAF engine)	
1784	**Bristol Scout**	1719	
2043	1611	1722	
		1735	
		1739	
		1758	
		2005	
		2010	
		2041	

No 10 Sqn	No 11 Sqn	No 16 Sqn	Aircraft Parks (Quantities held)	
BE2c	**Vickers**	**BE2c**		
(Renault engine)	**Gunbus**	(RAF engine)	**Avro 504A**	1
1674	1632	1705	**BE2b**	3
1682	1643	1707	**BE2c**	2
1789	1647	1712	(Renault engine)	
	1648	1717	**BE2c**	6
BE2c	1649	1731	(RAF engine)	
(RAF engine)	2866	2033	**Bristol Scout**	2
1708	2875	2037	**Caudron**	2
1715	2876		**FE2a**	1
1733	5454	**Maurice**	**Maurice Farman**	5
1737	5455	**Farman**	**Martinsyde**	2
2004		5004	**Morane**	3
2032		5015	**Vickers Gunbus**	4
2036		5019		
2044		5030		
2671		5036		
		Bristol Scout		
		4670		

NB: Nos 9, 12, 13, 14 and 15 Sqns had not reached the Front by this date.

Chapter 2

French and American bombers in British service

IN THE YEARS immediately preceding the First World War, France led the world in aviation, while America had the prestige of having originated the first flying machine. When war came Britain was soon denuded of aircraft in order to equip the initial squadrons of the British Expeditionary Force, and looked to both these two countries to supplement their needs until mid-1916 when British industry largely fulfilled the need.

Aircraft from France

Purchasing Commissions were set up in Paris by both the Royal Naval Air Service and the Royal Flying Corps. Some aircraft were bought on the spot in factories and contracts were made to produce others.

The French military aircraft were delivered in their national markings. These had been obligatory from an instruction issued on July 26 1912 by the French *Inspection Permante de l'Aeronautique* wherein it was decreed that aircraft wings would be marked with a *cocade* (roundel) 1 metre in outside diameter, that it would have a centre of blue of 40 centimetres diameter and an inner ring of white of 70 centimetres outside diameter. As related in Chapter 1, the British roundel was adopted from this, but with the colours reversed.

At that time, the roundel was such an innovation, with the issue confused by the Admiralty's original red ring marking, that the French marking was for a time accepted on the aircraft acquired. When it was pointed out that the colours were in the wrong order, it was often a case of painting over in the same proportions so that they were still not standard British roundels of the period. The French also used rudder striping; this was retained on French aircraft in British service since the order of colours, blue at the rudder post, red at the trailing edge and white in between, was the same in both services. It was not until 1930, as will be related, that the order of colours changed to be different from the French.

Another characteristic marking of French aircraft, often retained in British service, was the rudder serialling detail. Again this dated back to the 1912 instructions which also decreed that military aircraft would bear an initial letter on the rudder, indicative of the manufacturer, 30 centimetres high on both sides of the rudder, followed by the serial number of the aircraft in smaller 15-centimetre high characters. These measurements were not rigidly adhered to but, since they were mandatory before the *Inspection Permanente de l'Aeronautique* (the French equivalent of the British contemporary Aeronautical Inspection Department) would accept them for the Services, they were invariably marked together with load test figures in smaller markings. While these markings were often retained, a serial number was painted on the rear fuselage for identification in British service.

The rudder letters allotted to the French manufacturers producing aircraft in the early war years were BL for Bleriot, BRE for Brequet, C for Caudron, HF for Henri Farman, MF for Maurice Farman and V for Voisin, and examples of all these firms came to be used by the Royal Naval Air Service as bombers.

Representative examples are as follows:

British serial	Aircraft type	Original French No
1846	Maurice Farman Shorthorn	MF1049
1847	Bleriot Monoplane	BL1081
1851	Maurice Farman Shorthorn	MF1058
1852	Maurice Farman Shorthorn	MF1035
1853	Maurice Farman Shorthorn	MF1040
1856	Voisin Biplane	V240
1863	Morane	MS362
2863	Caudron GIII	C109
4299	Caudron GIII	C1887
5008	Maurice Farman Shorthorn	MF1699
5027	Maurice Farman Shorthorn	MF1664
5039	Morane Saulnier	MS424

It is at times difficult to draw a line between bombers and fighters in the early years of the 1914-18 War. Most reference books will include the Moranes as fighters and army co-operation aircraft, but it was as a bomber that the Morane first won fame. The German Army Zeppelin LZ37 was attacked and brought down by Flight Sub-Lieutenant Warneford at 03.00 hrs on June 7 1915; this was effected by dropping six 20 lb bombs from his Morane Parasol No 3253, when above the Zeppelin, one of which exploded within its envelope.

Nieuports and REPs (REP=Robert Esnault-Pelterie) were also used as

Figure 2   *(Figures given are diameter ratios.)*

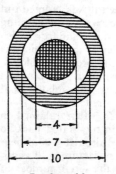
French roundel

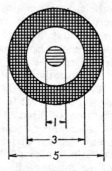
RNAS/RFC roundel

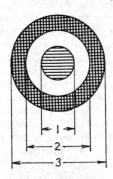
Current RAF roundel
(for comparison)

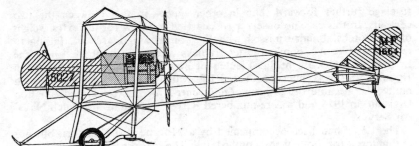

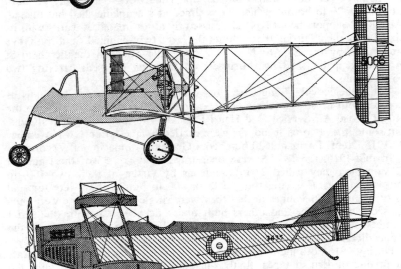

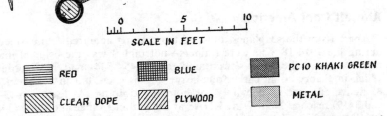

RED	BLUE	PC 10 KHAKI GREEN
CLEAR DOPE	PLYWOOD	METAL

Figure 3: *(Top) Maurice Farman with 80 hp Renault engine (No 48460/WD583) that served in France with No 16 Squadron mid-1916 and was flown to England October 20 1915 relegated to training duties. (Middle) Voisin with 140 hp Canton Unné engine that served in France with No 12 Squadron. Few of the Voisins used by the RFC served beyond 1915. (Bottom) Curtiss JN4 was essentially a trainer, but this American aircraft like the British Avro was adapted for bombing early in British service and several were used as bomber trainers capable of carrying four light bombs.*

bombers in 1915. The attack on the Zeebrugge seaplane sheds just before dawn on October 3 may be taken as typical. Flight Sub-Lieutenants Baudry and Hardstaff left Dunkirk Temporary Air Base in REP Parasols Nos 8461 and 8454 respectively, each carrying two 65 lb bombs. The aircraft bore British roundels on the full chord of the wings and on the

27

fuselage further forward than in other types—in fact between the two cockpits. In this case no observer was carried to allow for the extra weight of the bombs. Baudry missed with his bombs and Hardstaff, failing to reach his objective, bombed Ostend Docks where his bombs fell near the Ecluse de Chasse. Flight Sub-Lieutenant Boyd in REP No 8460 landed in Holland and was interned. The REP which had the original French number 59 became LA-23 in the *Luchtvaart Afdeling* (the Dutch Aviation Division) in 1916 and was re-numbered REP-3 in 1918 in the Dutch Naval Air Service.

The REPs had been accompanied by a Morane and Nieuport, but not as fighters—for both were bombed up. The Morane Parasol No 3244 carried six 20 lb bombs, which were aimed at a seaplane shed but missed. Also the Nieuport Scout No 8517 missed by an estimated 30 yards with its six 65 lb bombs. During that autumn the large twin-engined Caudron GIVs were used by the RNAS; Nos 3292 and 3294 attacked the Berchem St Agathe Zeppelin shed near Brussels on October 10, each carrying two 65 lb bombs.

While the Royal Flying Corps occasionally used Maurice Farmans as bombers but mostly for army co-operation work and then training, so the Royal Naval Air Service used Henri Farmans for spotting for naval guns, but sometimes two 65 lb bombs were carried by the latter. On November 28 1915, Henri Farman 3620 bombed a German submarine off Zeebrugge.

In mid-1916, the RNAS were operating a total of 32 of the Caudron GIVs which they called Twin Caudrons by virtue of their two 100 hp Anzani engines. Carrying four 65 lb or 100 lb bombs they were unusual as twin-engined machines in that they were single-seaters. Some were purchased from France and others built under licence in Britain; the serial numbers by which discrimination could be made are given in the Appendices.

During 1916 both the RFC and RNAS tended to discard French aircraft in favour of British types, firstly the Sopwith 1½ Strutter and later the DH4.

Aircraft from America

Apart from the seaplanes, most of the aircraft acquired from America during the 1914-18 War were trainers—not that it was the original intention. A hundred Curtiss R2s (numbered 3445-3544) had been ordered which in theory could carry four heavy bombs each, but in the event the 85 delivered were used mainly for bombing training. At least two (3455 and 3459) reached No 3 Wing RNAS at Luxieul in France and three (3462-3464) were shipped to the Aegean, but there are no records of them being used operationally. The RNAS classed them in 1918 as single-seat Heavy Bombers.

The famous Curtiss JN3s and JN4s, the standard American trainers, were also considered as bombing trainers and a few were fitted for dropping four 20 lb bombs.

All the American types were delivered in clear varnish finish and this practice was normally followed in British service. On some of the Curtisses the fuselage top-decking was given a khaki finish presumably as an anti-glare measure.

Chapter 3

Camouflage introduced

IN MID-1916 came the greatest and most fundamental change ever to affect the markings of British service aircraft, the introduction of camouflage. Not that forms of camouflage had not already been tried unofficially by some units. But now the standard 'colour', which had previously been natural linen, plain doped and varnished, was changed to a coloured finish, both as a means of camouflage and as a protective covering. This affected the application of all other markings.

Dope specifications and roundels

Hitherto, doping had been transparent to specifications decreed by the Royal Aircraft Factory. In 1916 instructions were issued that pigmented cellulose would be included as a final doping application, to upper and side surfaces to two approved specifications, PC10 or PC12, with a final protective transparent varnish. The purpose was two-fold, to meet a need to exclude the harmful actinic rays of the sun from damaging the fabric (best quality Irish linen at that time), and to assist in the concealment of aircraft dispersed on airfields.

Both approved protectives had lampblack as their colour base; with PC10 yellow ochre was added, and with PC12 red iron oxide, producing khaki-green and chocolate brown finishes respectively, if mixed in the intended proportions. Colour standards were not strictly adhered to and it is evident that a compromise mix was quite common. Under-surfaces were left natural linen as before, but with a final transparent varnish known as V114.

In general PC10 was usual for aircraft at home and PC12 overseas, the red oxide being more resistant to penetration by the sun's rays. Strangely, the RNAS favoured PC12 which was a camouflage more suited to land than sea, but no doubt the RFC in the field were quick to appreciate that, as a camouflage, the greenish PC10 was more suited to summer and the PC12 to winter.

National markings were by this time to a set standard that did not change until the Second World War, but when displayed on camouflaged surfaces it was usual to outline the roundel with a white 1-inch thick surround.

Whereas Second World War roundel outlining was yellow and varied

29

in thickness in 2 inch stages from 2 to 6 inches on bombers, in the First World War the outlining was white and invariably of 1 inch thickness irrespective of roundel diameter. Furthermore, unlike the Second World War period when roundel size was conditioned to 54 inches diameter maximum, the First World War diameter was in many cases conditioned only by the size of the wing chord.

Squadron markings remained unchanged in form but, of course, the black bars introduced on the BE bombing and reconnaissance aircraft in April 1916 to denote their squadrons as depicted in Chapter 1 had to be changed to white on the new darkened surfaces.

Serials

Hitherto numbers had been marked black on British service aircraft, but on the new camouflaged surfaces this did not show up. Some manufacturers, nevertheless, persisted in painting the numbers black. Others outlined the black letters in white, while Sopwiths commenced using a white rectangular box at the rear of the fuselage for their numbering, and left the fin in clear dope carrying their trade name. Other firms changed the number presentation to white, but the Aircraft Manufacturing Company, producing De Havilland designs, followed the practice of painting serials on the rudder stripes.

Different firms, then, had characteristic ways of presenting their serial marking, which was not standardised as in the Second World War, and one aircraft type could be produced by more than ten different contractors. It is not always appreciated, incidentally, that there were more plants in Britain producing complete airframes in the First World War than in the Second.

Apart from their presentation the character of the serial numbers was changing. When 10000 was reached prefix letters were introduced, and numbers started again at No 1, prefixed by the letter 'A'. First machines with numbers in the new series were a batch of aircraft used as bombers— FE2ds 'A1' to 'A40'. The first, delivered in mid-1916, had Rolls-Royce Eagle engine I/250/7WD6149 (ie, the 7th Mk I 250 hp Rolls-Royce with the War Department engine serial number 6149) and served in No 20 Squadron until captured by the Germans on May 7 1917.

However, while RFC aircraft were numbered in a 1-9999 range with A, B, D and E prefixes, RNAS aircraft were given an N prefix thereby making a clear distinction between military and naval aircraft.

Ex-fighter bomber types

Typical of the make-shift bombers of the mid-war years, both the BE12 (basically a re-engined single-seat BE2c) and the Martinsyde Elephant were initially ordered and produced as fighters, at which task they were found wanting so were subsequently used as bombers. Both types had clear finishes on initial production and were camouflaged with PC10 later, either in production or in service.

The introduction of camouflage initially brought anomalies which were manifest on these bombers of 1916. It was not unusual for squadrons to hold uncamouflaged and camouflaged aircraft, and even single aircraft with some components in dark finish and others in light.

The Martinsyde Elephants were of two types—the G100 and G102 with 120 and 160 hp Beardmore engines respectively. Their serial numbers were a guide to the type as given in the Appendices.

Squadron examples include: 7301 of No 27 Squadron which landed in German lines on July 9 1916 when Sub-Lieutenant R. W. Nicholl was taken prisoner; 7481, the second of the 80 victims of von Richthofen on September 23 1916; A1600 of 22 Reserve Squadron, Egypt, in September 1917; A3978 'B4' of No 27 Squadron shot down near Quesnoy on August 9 1917; A6286, a presentation aircraft, marked RHODESIA III.

The BE12s were converted to various standards for which no serial guide exists, but serial numbers are a guide to the particular constructor as detailed in the Appendices.

Squadron examples include: 6172 delivered new from St Omer to No 19 Squadron, September 27 1916; 6646 served in No 21 Squadron until 1.10 pm January 28 1917, when shot down by anti-aircraft fire; A4007 served No 17 Squadron and A4008 in No 47 Squadron in Salonika.

The FE2b and 2d

These two pusher aircraft types were introduced as fighters, but were used mainly as bombers and bomber reconnaissance aircraft. By their very configuration they were in a class apart for markings. Roundels were placed on the nacelle and were invariably small. Since there was insufficient fin area for the serial number to be displayed, these were in 8-inch high numbers across the rudder stripes.

An important marking innovation with the FEs was night camouflage. While the experimental station at Orfordness conducted official experiments, some units evolved their own unofficial night camouflage. No 100 Squadron with FE2bs, assigned to night bombing, painted one of their machines jet black and later others were similarly treated.

As a general rule FE2as had 100 hp Green engines and were delivered in plain dope; only a few were built. The FE2ds had 250 hp Rolls-Royce engines with the serials 7995, A'1-40, A'1932-1966, A'5143-5152, all built by the Royal Aircraft Factory and marked as printed with the apostrophe in the serial, and A6351-6570 and B1851-1900 built by Boulton & Paul. The remainder (and bulk) of the FEs were FE2bs with 120 hp or 160 hp Beardmore engines.

Squadron examples include: FE2b 4917, which served in No 18 Squadron until August 5 1916 when it was hit by anti-aircraft fire, then fired on by a Fokker monoplane and finally crashed on landing; FE2b 5201, a presentation aircraft marked BOMBAY No 1, built by Boulton & Paul and first flown on October 2 1915 with 120 hp Beardmore engine 277/WD1341 fitted; it was flown to France on October 10 1915 and delivered to No 16 Squadron ten days later; FE2b 6348 built by the Royal Aircraft Factory and operated by No 23 Squadron until lost on June 26 1916; FE2b A822 which was painted black—it was set on fire by its No 100 Squadron crew who had started out to bomb Gontrode Zeppelin shed, but had been forced down on a ploughed field in enemy territory after the engine had been damaged by anti-aircraft fire; FE2d A'5 which landed at Lille in German-held territory June 1 1916 while on its delivery flight to

31

France; FE2d A39 which was the No 20 Squadron aircraft in which Sergeant T. Mottershead won his VC; D9117 which was built by G & J Weir and served in No 148 Squadron; and D9998 which was built by Ransome, Sims & Jeffries and served in No 102 Squadron.

First 'true' bomber

The Sopwith 1½ Strutter was the first of the 'true' bombers. It was produced in two versions, a two-seat fighter with a capacity for dropping four light bombs, known as Admiralty Type 9400, and a single-seat bomber version known as Admiralty Type 9700; the type number was conditioned by the standard of the particular aircraft that bore these serial numbers.

While the initial deliveries to the Services were aircraft in plain doped finish in early 1916, all 1½ Strutter deliveries from June were camouflaged. Sopwith continued to keep the fins in a clear doped finish to permit the presentation of the firm's name and address, and the serial number was entered on a white box background that became a characteristic of Sopwith-built aircraft. There were some transfers of RNAS aircraft to the RFC with consequent changes in serial number, eg, 9681 going to No 70 Squadron RFC as A891. A number of 1½ Strutters bore presentation details but these were appropriate to the 9400 fighter versions, not the bombers.

Squadron markings of 1½ Strutters were of two distinct types according to service in RFC or RNAS. Since most of those delivered to the RFC went to fighter squadrons, the survey is limited to those of Nos 3 and 5 Wings RNAS which used the 1½ Strutters as bombers and bomber escorts.

No 3 Wing based on Luxeuil, with a forward base for mounting operations at Ochey, in the province Lorraine, was the world's first 'strategic air force' and conducted operations against German industry from late 1916 to early 1917. Rarely does documentary evidence exist of the change in camouflage or whether brown or green dope was used, but No 3 Wing is the exception. A note from Lt E. R. Peal, the Wing's Engineering Officer, to Wing Commander R. B. Davies at Ochey on November 25 1916 runs:

'Submitted,

May I be advised how the fabric is lasting on the fuselages of machines which have been repaired and covered at the Depot, on which varnish has been used and not brown dope. Also whether you would prefer that machines taken into Depot for repair are left white or brown. A sufficiency of brown dope is at last to hand.'

From this it is evident that the depot in re-covering airframes had been using clear dope with a protective varnish. Davies' reply has not been traced but he was evidently in favour of the camouflaged dope being used as photographs verify.

Some 1½ Strutters in this Wing had individual motifs on the fuselage side in red, blue, yellow and white based on naval signal code flags, and in some cases these were repeated on the tailplane. All had individual Wing numbers painted on fuselage sides as shown in the table on page 33.

Both Nos 4 and 5 Wings operated Sopwith 1½ Strutter bombers from bases in the Dunkirk area. Examples of these operating with No 5 Wing are 9394, 9395, 9397, N5081 and N5114.

CAMOUFLAGE INTRODUCED

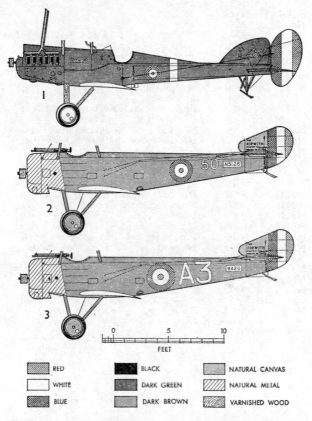

Figure 4: *(1) A BE12 of No 37 Training Depot Station, Yatesbury. From its name OMBRA, marked on the fuselage just aft of the engine, it is possible it was used by No 32 (Australian Flying Corps) Training Squadron at Yatesbury. (2) Sopwith 1½ Strutter (Type 9700) of No 3 Wing RNAS, as it appeared March 4 1917 flown by Flight Sub-Lieutenant Masson during a raid on Brebach. (3) Sopwith 1½ Strutter of No 5 Wing which was interned after landing in neutral Holland on September 17 1916 and became LA38 (later S24) in the Dutch Army Air Arm.*

The following is a listing of Sopwith 1½ Strutters with No 3 Wing, Ochey, January 1917, for strategic bombing operations.

Fuselage No	Serial No	Type No	Remarks
1	N5088	9700	Went to French Air Force
2	9706	9700	Collected from Luxeuil, December 16 1916
3	9657	9700	Serviceable
4	9661	9700	Sent to Luxeuil for repair, January 17 1917
5	9711	9700	Serviceable
6	9667	9400	Marked TIENTSIN BRITONS No 2*
7	9669	9700	Participated in Brebach raid, March 4 1917
8	9738	9700	Serviceable
10	9742	9700	Flown by Flt Cdr C. D. Draper
12	9744	9400	Marked BRITONS IN ITALY No 1*

33

Fuselage No	Serial No	Type No	Remarks
19	9722	9400	Marked SAO PAULO BRITONS No 1 *
20	9708	9400	Short range version of 9400
21	9733	9700	Believed lost in January 1917
23	9651	9700	First built to contract CP104237/16
24	N5091	9700	Handed over to French Air Force
25	N5089	9700	Serviceable
28	9735	9400	Serviceable
29	9730	9400	Force landed, December 3 1916
30	9700	9700	Prototype of bomber series
32	N5098	9700	Handed over to French Air Force
34	N5104	9700	Handed over to French Air Force
35	N5106	9700	Serviceable
36	N5107	9700	Damaged January 1917
37	N5109	9700	Damaged January 1917
38	N5121	9700	Destroyed January 1917
39	N5122	9700	Handed over to French Air Force
41	9410	9400	Short-range version of 9400
43	N5116	9700	Handed over to French Air Force
44	N5115	9700	Handed over to French Air Force
46	N5171	9700	Flown by Wg Cdr Rathbone
48	N5123	9700	Handed over to French Air Force
49	N5128	9700	Handed over to French Air Force
50	N5126	9700	To French Air Force (airframe only)
51	N5173	9400	Short-range version of 9400
53	N5174	9400	Replacement RIO DE JANEIRO BRITONS No 1 *
54	N5124	9700	Serviceable

* Presentation machines

34

Chapter 4

The de Havilland day bombers—
DH4 and DH9

THE DH4 was the first aircraft, designed specifically as a day bomber, to be put into large-scale production. It was followed by the DH9 which, although committed to large-scale production, was no great improvement on the DH4 until re-engined as the DH9A. Finally, there was the DH10 twin-engined day bomber that arrived too late to see operations. The activities of the DH4 and DH9 were largely restricted to war-time, and those of the DH9A and DH10 to the post-war period; this chapter is concerned with the DH4 and DH9.

General finish

With the DH4 it was a case of its construction conditioning its basic colouring. Most aircraft up to this time were wooden structures, fabric covered; but the DH4 had the forward fuselage covered in ply. As a result, in 1916, before camouflage was universal in the Services, the prototype and early production models had clear doped fabric on wings and rear fuselage, with polished ply forward. On the camouflaged finishes of bulk production machines, the PC10/PC12 finishes in khaki green and chocolate brown were usual for main and tailplane upper-surfaces and rear fuselage, with the plywood forward surfaces covered in paints to specifications X16 and X2, a grey undercoat and battleship grey finishing coat respectively.

Although camouflage was in general use by the time DH4 production was under way, a number of early DH4s were turned out in clear finish for sheer lack of the necessary pigmented dopes. Adequate supplies had been provisioned but on the scale of 20% PC10 to the clear dopes Cellon NP2 or Emaillite 11A, on the understanding that if five coats of doping were necessary to achieve the necessary tautness of the fabric, only the last coat would be in PC10. As it was, many units were using the PC10 for all coatings and so exhausting stocks. In fact, on January 25 1917 the Naval Stores Officer at Sheerness, responsible for provisioning RNAS units in South-East England, reported a nil stock of PC10 and could issue only clear dopes. Such a situation is an early example of many to come in bombing colours—the disparity between what was laid down for the colour and markings, and what was actually applied.

The first squadron to equip with the DH4 was No 55, with which Captain W. E. Johns, subsequently author of the famous 'Biggles' stories, gained much of his first-hand experience. The squadron was based in France behind the British Front from March to October 1917, then it moved to Ochey, near Nancy, to join No 41 Wing, the forerunner of the Independent Air Force. While there an American officer, sent by the Air Service, American Expeditionary Force, to report on the 'Preservation of Airplanes', visited No 55 Squadron and its Wing Depot, No 6 Air Park, to report on the finish of the aircraft and their weathering. This was in connection with the DH4s the Americans were themselves producing.

There has been much controversy on the precise shade of the colouring of dopes on 1914-18 aircraft, and opinions have been expressed in several books while artists have translated these opinions in colour. Some have said that the khaki-green was a fallacy and all were khaki-brown. It is pointless to ask the survivors of that war, for the mind is not retentive of shades. Here, no further opinions are given, but relevant extracts from the report of the American officer concerned at the time, promulgated by the Chief of Air Service, American Expeditionary Force on May 25 1918, are interesting.

'The experience of the British at Dunkerque, Ochey, No 6 Air Park and No 55 Squadron has been valuable and indicates that the following coatings gave satisfactory results:

(i) To the linen fabric apply 6 coats of "Raftight". This is a colourless dope. Next apply 2 finishing coats of "PC10"; this is an olive green dope, sometimes called "Khaki Paint".

(ii) To the linen fabric apply 3 coats of Cellon, a transparent dope. Next 2 finishing coats of PC10 Emaillite, an olive green dope.

The second method is preferred by the Air Park men as it adds less to the weight of the plane and gives a satisfactory surface. The first method is said to be used because of a shortage of Cellon.'

'Raftight' was the name for 'RAF tightener' (ie, dope—the initials standing for Royal Aircraft Factory). Cellon and Emaillite were proprietary dopes to official specifications.

Of RNAS squadrons using the DH4, the report had this to say:

'The opinion of those using faster planes, such as the DH4, was that an additional coat or two of varnish over the PC10, gives the fabric a smoother surface, tending to cut down skin friction. Therefore, for the fast land machines at least it can be said that the use of varnish certainly has its advantages in giving added protection against weather and a smoother, better surface. The only disadvantages are that it adds slightly to the weight and cost and makes the planes show up a little more prominently when turning in the sunlight, due to reflected light from the highly finished surfaces'.

Thus camouflage was sacrificed for speed, a vital factor in day bomber squadrons, which at times had to fight their way both to and from their targets. In effect, their khaki-green surfaces had a sheen.

The painting of the DH9 followed much on the lines of the DH4, except that in many cases the plywood was painted in khaki-green or chocolate brown to match the fabric doping.

17 *DH9 in No 211 Squadron, RAF, with the identification letter 'A' made into an individual name* (via Bryan Philpott).

18 *In service use. A Westland-built DH4 marked B2 in No 5 Wing, RNAS. The '5' indicating the wing can be seen adjacent to the roundel* (J. M. Bruce/G. S. Leslie Collection).

19 *Pilots and observers in DH4, DH9 and DH9A squadrons, unlike fighter pilots, did not appear to object to having the target-like roundel marked by their cockpits. This photograph was actually taken at midnight—in North Russia, 1919.*

20 *Early production DH4s surviving in 1918 often found their way into training units with some transition in markings. See close-up view and further detail below* (via J. T. C. Long).

21 *A7783 shown here and above has the typical serial presentation of the Aircraft Manufacturing Company, but is without a fuselage roundel. As an instructor's aircraft in No 44 Training Squadron, it bears the names of two instructors, but evidently it had been flown by a pupil on February 3 1918 when this photo was taken* (via J. T. C. Long).

22 *Post-war finish; a DH4A (converted Palladium Autocars DH4 airframe) used for communications work with a passenger cabin added.*

23 *DH9 with a Napier Lion engine (an installation applicable to J6957-6962); aircraft in aluminium finish overall* (Real Photographs 1811).

24 *Handley Page 0/100 with typical large roundels taking the full wing chord and with rudder striping occupying the whole rudder area.*

25 *Handley Page 0/400 with standardised small roundels and rudder flashes. Note the fine white outline to both flash and roundels. There are no roundels under the lower wings (G. S. Leslie/J. M. Bruce Collection).*

26 *Handley Page 0/400 of No 207 Squadron. Aircraft were lettered 'A', 'B' or 'C' according to flight in the squadron, with Nos 1 to 6 in each case.*

27 *Handley Page 0/400, D8345, trundles in to land over the tree tops. Note that the 'D' of the serial is superimposed on the tail flash over the white/red sections.*

39

28 *Captured—Lieut Vereker's 0/100 with its roundels superseded by Iron Crosses. The 'Lift here' marking is retained and can just be seen* (H. J. Nowarra).

29 *An exception to the rule. An 0/100 with large roundels outlined in white* (G. S. Leslie/J. M. Bruce Collection).

30 *Rear view showing positioning of the serial at the extreme end of the fuselage—a practice exclusive to and consistent with Handley Page bombers. Photo also shows that rudder flashes appeared on both sides of each rudder* (G. S. Leslie/J. M. Bruce Collection).

31 *Handley Page V/1500, evidently a brand new machine, with rudder striping but devoid of roundel or serial.*

Unit markings

As day bombers, DH4s and DH9s serving on the Western Front came into the general scheme of squadron markings, of simple geometrical symbols as follows:

Sqn	Aircraft	Marking aft of roundel
18	DH4	18 in white square
25	DH4	White crescent
27	DH4	White vertical bar
49	DH4	White dumbell
57	DH4	White disc
98	DH9	White zig-zag
103	DH9	White slanting bars

On March 21 1918 the Germans launched their last great offensive, causing disruption on the Western Front, followed by a planned reshuffle of units to reinforce threatened areas. Among the many counter-measures taken was a decree by the Royal Flying Corps for the obliteration of all squadron markings on Corps Reconnaissance and Day Bombing aircraft.

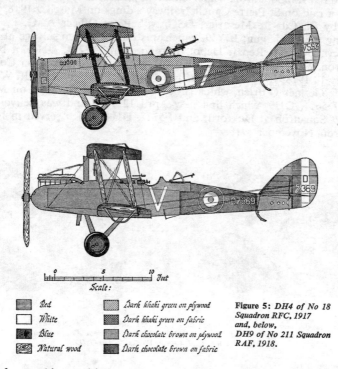

Red	Dark khaki green on plywood
White	Dark khaki green on fabric
Blue	Dark chocolate brown on plywood
Natural wood	Dark chocolate brown on fabric

Scale: 0 5 10 Feet

Figure 5: DH4 of No 18 Squadron RFC, 1917 and, below, DH9 of No 211 Squadron RAF, 1918.

Thus the markings tabled were not applicable after March 22 1918. The object of this measure was to deny German intelligence an estimate of the reshuffle of forces from examples shot down. (On fighters, squadron markings were retained but changed to confuse enemy intelligence.) Individual letters or figures and flight markings continued to be marked as before.

That is on the fuselage side, on the nose or aft of the roundel, and often repeated in white on the top wing and in black on the bottom wing. In No 55 Squadron an unusual embellishment for the period was the painting of wheel discs red, white and blue for the respective 'A', 'B' and 'C' Flights.

Serial markings

The DH4 and DH9 were widely subcontracted and the various constructors each had their own techniques in finishing the aircraft and these became manifest in two ways. Firstly by the manufacturers' own trade marking and secondly by the method they employed in marking the aircraft's official serial number. However, local instructions by the RFC on the Western Front decreed from February 1 1918 that manufacturers' names should not be marked. DH4 and DH9 serial numbers spanned the First World War range from 'A' to 'H' prefixes. Examples of individual aircraft include: A8000, DH4 of No 18 Sqn, crashed in forced landing after an air combat, May 25, 1918—the crew were uninjured; B7591, DH9 of No 6 (Naval) Squadron, which shook off an attack by 6 Albatros Scouts during a raid on St Pierre Capelle railway sidings on March 9 1918, when flown by Flt Cdr Le Mesurier, DSC, with Petty Officer A. G. L. Ryan manning the Lewis gun; B7749, which was built up from salvage at No 1 (Southern) Aircraft Repair Depot, Farnborough; A7781, DH4, of No 55 Squadron, which shot down an Albatros Scout out of control over Cologne on May 18 1918; B7596, a DH9 of No 206 Sqn, flown by Lt L. R. Warren and Air Gunner O'Brien, which shot down an Albatros Scout on May 3 1918; D5611, DH9, which first flew April 12 1918 and was delivered to No 119 Squadron at Duxford; and F5727, DH4, which served in No 57 Squadron, November 1918.

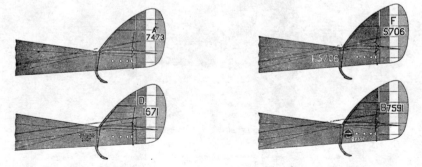

Figure 6: *Manufacturers' stylings in factory finish: (A7473) Aircraft Manufacturing Company, Hendon (DH4); (D1671) Mann, Egerton Ltd, Norwich (DH9); (F5706) Palladium Autocars Ltd, Putney (DH4); and (B7591) Westland Aircraft Works, Yeovil (DH9).*

Chapter 5

The Handley Page night bombers—
0/100, 0/400 and V/1500

FIRST OF THE TWIN-ENGINED heavy bombers to go into regular service, the Handley Page bomber was conceived by the Air Dept of the Admiralty as a 'bloody paralyser'. The prototype Handley Page 0/100 emerged in 1915 as the largest aircraft ever built in Britain. On December 9 1915 it was moved by road from the firm's Cricklewood works to Hendon, where it made a short first flight on December 17.

The prototype 0/100 was in clear doped fabric finish, with its serial 1455 marked in small black digits at the extreme rear of the fuselage. The second prototype, with a lengthened nose, which flew on April 23 1916, was similarly finished, but with the number 1456. Nos 1457-1466 of the initial order for 12 followed at intervals, but by the time they reached units, the khaki PC10 pigmented cellulose dope was the standard finish. The prototype, brought up later to production standard, was redoped khaki for service in No 16 (Naval) Squadron.

Roundels borne by Handley Page 0/100s were the largest ever to appear on British service aeroplanes, by virtue of the fact that they were marked over the full wing chord and fuselage depth of the then largest aeroplane in service.

The first service unit of 0/100s was known simply as 'The Handley Page Squadron'; the commanding officer, Sqn Cdr J. Babington, took office on August 4 1916. Aircraft Nos 1458-1461 were allotted and No 1460 was the first to fly to France in October 1916. When No 1461 followed it force landed at Abbeville with engine trouble and Babington issued a warning about maintenance, pointing out that in this case the aircraft had landed safely in our own territory. There was a fear that an example of Britain's giant bomber might fall into enemy hands—and this is precisely what did happen some weeks later, and in consequence the Handley Page concerned had its roundels changed to black crosses.

It happened like this. The 0/100 left England at 11.30 hrs on January 1 1917 with pilot, observer and three mechanics. Over the Channel, fog was experienced and the pilot, Lt Vereker, took the aircraft up to get above it —and ran into a thunderstorm. This upset the compass and the pilot decided to turn back. The weather deteriorated further and the machine was brought down with the intention of landing as soon as suitable land was sighted. After noting a church steeple when flying at 150 feet the pilot put the Handley Page down into an adjacent field. The crew then set out to walk to the nearest telephone to get aid—only to find they were made captive having landed in enemy territory near Laon. Since the Germans intended a flight test evaluation of their prize, the roundels were obliterated and black crosses applied. Exactly six months earlier one of the first FE2ds (A9) had flown straight from Farnborough to land in enemy territory south-west of Lille.

In early 1917 a few 0/100s reached No 3 Wing but were later withdrawn and together with others from England entered service with No 5 Wing, RNAS. After daylight bombing operations against enemy destroyers in which No 3115, the first of the second order for 0/100s, came down in the sea off Ostend, operations were confined to night attacks. An exception was in September 1917 when four were withdrawn for a short period to Redcar for daylight anti-submarine operations. Four 100 lb bombs were dropped from 3123 on September 21 on a German U-boat seen lying on the sea bed in clear water, but without any result.

By the time the Handley Page had been put into large-scale production as the 0/400 with a modified fuel system and detail improvements, a standardised finishing scheme was evolved and the drawings on page 45 show the two standards. As always, there were some exceptions to the general rulings.

Exclusive type markings

An unusual feature, exclusive to Handley Page aircraft products 1915-19, was the positioning of the serial number at the extreme rear of the fuselage; in black on early uncamouflaged machines and in white on those with khaki finish. An unusual feature of the 0/400s, and almost exclusive to these bombers, was a rudder flash not unlike the fin flash of today. The change from rudder striping to a small flash was evidently for the same reason as the change from large to small roundels; that the large white area of the national colours was deemed to compromise camouflage. In the Second World War history was to repeat itself on this aspect of bombing colours.

There was yet another and completely new type of marking that was exclusive to the large Handley Pages—night handling markings. It was often necessary to have the aircraft turned into wind for take-off or turned after landing. To ensure that ground handling parties at night, lifting the tail to swing the aircraft round, applied lift on a member of the structure and not on unsupported fabric, the appropriate points were suitably emphasised with thick white lines.

Even pilot's individual markings were presented on positions exclusive to the type since, apart from limited use of Caudron GIVs, the 0/100s and 0/400s were the only twin-engined bombers to be operated during the war by the RFC and RNAS. These markings were placed centrally on the tip of the nose. The style had been set in the autumn of 1917 when No 3123, the 0/100 mentioned above, was stationed at Redcar. The pilot, Flight Lieutenant L. G. Sieveking, DSC, was generally regarded as hamfisted with anything except a control column. Thus, the nose of his aircraft bore a hand-painted splay-fingered fist, with Sieveking's nickname 'SPLIT-PIN'

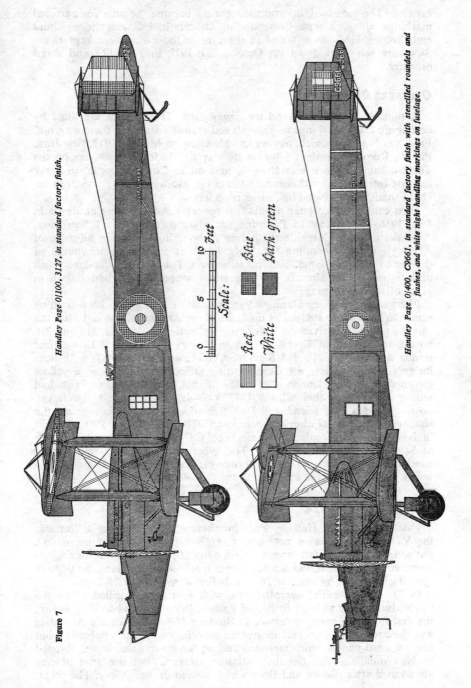

Figure 7

Handley Page 0/100, 3127, in standard factory finish.

Handley Page 0/400, C9661, in standard factory finish with stencilled roundels and flashes, and white night handling markings on fuselage.

Scale:

0 5 10 Feet

Red

Blue

White

Dark green

beneath. The idea took on and the nose tip became the area for personal markings, although some Commanding Officers had different ideas about embellishing HM aircraft and in these units the noses were kept clean. Sieveking was shot down on October 31 1917 in No 3123 and taken prisoner.

Overseas 0/400s

A number of 0/400s found their way East. They can be classified by describing their markings as they staged through Italy on their way out. First was No 3124 which, having left Manston on May 23 1917, flew from Pisa to Rome seven days later on its way to Mudros for attacks on the Turkish ships *Goeben* and *Breslau,* and on to Constantinople, to make the first inter-continental bombing attacks in history. It was finished in the khaki shade of PC10 and had large roundels.

Next came a much later production model, C9681, staging at Rome in July 1918 on its way to Palestine for attachment to No 1 Squadron, Australian Flying Corps. Participating in bombing attacks in advance of Allenby's troops liberating the Holy Land, it earned the nickname of 'Father of all Aeroplanes' by local tribesmen. This had the standard finish of late production aircraft with the small roundels and rudder flash in place of rudder striping.

Plans to establish ten Handley Page squadrons in Egypt with a training centre in Crete were shelved at the time of the Armistice, but just after the war the plan was revived on a more modest scale and Nos 58, 214 and 216 Squadrons moved to Egypt. In general these were all in drab wartime standard finish, but No 214 Squadron enlivened their aircraft with nose insignia. Appropriately the Commanding Officer's machine had a yellow crown on the nose, denoting his badge of rank—Major. Lesser lights had motifs according to their whims; D8323 displayed an ivy leaf, significant, no doubt, of a lady friend and D4578 bore a terrier. Unfortunately the squadron lost several aircraft en route; C9714, D4591 and F304 crashed in July 1919 and a replacement machine, C9743, was destroyed in a gale at St Raphael the same month. The other two squadrons had similar troubles and Lawrence of Arabia broke his arm when D5439 in which he was a passenger crashed en route to the Middle East.

The Super Handleys

Last of the line of Handley Page bombers of the First World War was the V/1500 which was a new design, embodying features of the 0/400, but apart from being four-engined with pairs of pusher and tractor engines mounted in tandem, it was a much larger machine outspanning the 0/400's spread of 100 feet by another 26 feet. It first flew on May 25 1918.

PC10 was the initial overall finish, with roundels stencilled as on the 0/400, but rudder striping in lieu of flashes. Intended for bombing Berlin, the first few were entering service at Bircham Newton when the Armistice was declared. Squadron and individual markings were not applicable, but two acquired names which were painted on the nose. *Atlantic* was shipped to Newfoundland for the first Atlantic air race, but the attempt was abandoned after Alcock and Brown had crossed in their Vimy. The other, marked HMA *Carthusian,* made the first through flight to India in December 1918. During 1919 most surviving V/1500s were placed in store.

At the end of the war night bombers were being subjected to a new camouflage finish, resulting from experiments carried out in 1918, that set the style for post-war years.

Civil service

While the Handley Page 0/400 may be thought of as essentially a bomber, it is a fact that it was the first of the airliners and Certificates of Airworthiness Nos 1 to 4, issued on May 1 1919, were to Handley Page 0/400s. The distinction of bearing the letters G-EAAA went to a DH9— but that was not an airliner.

These first British civil airliners were owned by their makers who formed a subsidiary company, Handley Page Air Transport Ltd. Perhaps the term 'airliner' is something of an overstatement for they were hurried conversions by removing all military attachments, repositioning some equipment and introducing wicker chairs and side-seats into the draughty, noisy, windowless cabin, and blanking over the dorsal gun position.

Their first payload was ten passengers conveyed from Cricklewood to Alexandra Park Aerodrome at Manchester on May 4 1919. Cricklewood, the Handley Page airfield, was conveniently nearer to the centre of London than the present London airport at Heathrow. The aircraft was flown on this occasion by the company's chief test pilot, Lieutenant-Colonel W. F. Sholto Douglas—the late Lord Douglas of Kirtleside. At this time the aircraft still wore their military finish, and were doped overall in the AMA scheme of three coats of this pigmented cellulose which dried a matt dark chocolate brown on the fabric, to which was added one coat of transparent varnish giving a smoother finish and a slight sheen. As regards identification marks, there was a curious situation. The official register was purely provisional pending international decisions, and aircraft operated with their service identity numbers marked large on the fuselage side in white to contrast with the drab brown. The 0/400s concerned were D8350, F5414, F5418 and F5417 which later became G-EAAE, F, G and W respectively.

One of the stipulations of the International Convention on Civil Aviation in July 1919 was that the nationality characters, represented by Roman capital letters, G for Great Britain, should be painted on both sides of the rudder or (as was the case with the Handley Page) on the outer sides of the outer rudders, if more than one was fitted. Accordingly the outer rudder surfaces were marked with a large white square as a background for a large black 'G'. On F5414 and F5417 a further step was taken of changing the fuselage lettering from the style F5414 to G-5414.

By that time, Handley Page had introduced an improved version of the aircraft, designated the 0/7. These were 14-seaters with an appointed cabin from which the fuel tanks had to be removed and placed in extended nacelles behind each engine. Windows of Triplex were incorporated, more for lighting than for viewing. The first conversion initially flew marked just HP1. From this aircraft onward the firm instituted a system of fleet numbers and earlier machines were included down the list. These numbers, prefixed HP, were marked at the rear of the fuselage where Handley Page had once marked their official RAF service serials.

By the end of 1919 the tenets of the International Convention were fully operative. Decrees affecting civil aircraft markings were as follows:

'The nationality and registration marks on flying machines shall be painted in black on a white ground in the following manner: The marks shall be painted once on the lower surface of the lower main plane and once on the upper surface of the top main planes, the tops of the letters to be towards the leading edge. They shall also be painted along each side of the fuselage between the mainplanes and the tailplanes. The nationality mark (ie the letter G in this case) shall also be painted on the left and right sides of the lower surface of the lowest tailplanes or elevators whichever is the larger (the tailplane in the Handley Page's case).

'The height of the marks on the mainplanes and tailplanes shall be equal to four-fifths of the chord.

'The height of the marks on the fuselage shall be four-fifths of the depth of the narrowest part of that portion of the fuselage on which the marks are painted.

'The nationality and registration marks need not exceed 2.5 metres in height. The width of the letters shall be two-thirds of their height and the thickness shall be one-sixth of their height. The letters shall be painted in plain black type and shall be uniform in shape and size. A space equal to half width of letters shall be left between the letters. A hyphen of a length equal to the width of one of the letters shall be painted between the nationality mark and the registration mark.'

So marked, the Handley Pages were the progenitors of the airliners of today, with domestic and continental services. By the late spring of 1920, after a year of operation, they had carried 4,614 passengers in the UK and 1,413 on continental trips. Other countries were interested and seven 0/7s were supplied to China. Two variants of the 0/7 were made, an 0/10 12-passenger version and an 0/11 passenger/freighter type; in the latter the freight was carried amidships with a small cabin for two forward and a cabin for three aft.

The most embellished of the early Handleys was G-EANV which was used for advertising when flown in South Africa. Its large surfaces were used as hoardings in an advertising campaign. The fuselage sides, between main and tailplanes, were painted with the word COMMANDO. The under-surface of the lower plane was painted white and bore the black letters COMM (starboard) and ANDO (port), while the under-surfaces of the top wing overhang, with white patches, bore the words COMMANDO (starboard) and BRANDY (port). Having flown to South Africa this aircraft was deservedly named PIONEER which was marked on the side of the nose in white, for apart from the large white lettering backgrounds it was still in wartime AMA doping scheme.

Apart from the civil airline operated by Handley Page with their own aircraft types, the Royal Air Force operated their own airline—the 86th (Communications) Wing formed in December 1918 to convey officials to and from the Peace Conference at Versailles. The aircraft used were DH4s and Handley Page 0/400s converted for passenger-carrying. They were in two squadrons — No 1 (Communications) initially at Hendon, with a detachment at Buc in France which expanded into No 2 (Communications) whereupon No 1 moved to Kenley. The HP 0/400s operated by the Wing differed from standard service machines in interior seating arrangements and an enlarged Triplex window; but visually they differed greatly, with an overall aluminium dope that contrasted with the drab camouflage of the period. Appropriately, the aircraft bore names prefixed by 'Silver' in the manner HMA (for His Majesty's Aircraft) *Silver Queen*. The Wing disbanded in September 1919 and the following year the Handley Page wartime bomber conversions for civil use were being withdrawn in favour of a specially designed type—the W8.

Handley Page 0/400 civil conversions

HP Fleet No	Civil registration	Original service serial	HP Type No	Remarks (individual names where applicable given in italics)
1	G-EAGN	C9704	0/7	Prototype 0/7. Allotted K-162. Marked HP1
7	G-EANV		0/7	*Commando*. Crashed in South Africa February 23 1920
10	G-EAQZ		0/7	Sold, presumed abroad, 1920
11	G-EAPA		0/7	Sold, presumed abroad, 1920
12	G-EAPB		0/7	Sold, presumed abroad, 1920
13	G-EEAF	F5414	0/7	Originally flew as 0/400. Withdrawn August 1920
14	G-EAAW	F5417	0/400	Withdrawn from service April 1920
15	G-EAPJ	C9713	0/400	Parts used for first W8
16	G-EAAE	D8350	0/400	*Vulture*. Withdrawn from service August 1920
18	G-EEAG	F5418	0/400	*Penguin*. Withdrawn from service April 1920
19	G-EAKF	J2259	0/400	Withdrawn from service late 1920
20	G-EAKG	J2250	0/400	Withdrawn from service mid-1920
21	G-EALX	J2251	0/400	Withdrawn from service in 1920
22	G-EAKE	J2252	0/400	Crashed in Sweden, June 1920
23	G-EALZ	J2243	0/400	Withdrawn from service late 1920
24	G-EALY	J2247	0/400	Withdrawn from service in 1920
25	G-EAMA	J2248	0/400	Crashed near Golders Green, December 14 1920
26	G-EAMB	D4623	0/400	Withdrawn from service in 1920
27	G-EAMC	D4624	0/400	Crashed in Sudan, February 25 1920
28	G-EAMD	D4633	0/400	Sold to Polish Government in 1920
30	G-EASL	C9699	0/11	Withdrawn from service April 1921
31	G-EASM	C9731	0/11	Withdrawn from service April 1921
32	G-EASN	C4611	0/11	Withdrawn from service April 1921
33	G-EASO	D5444	0/400	*Old Carthusian II*. Napier Lion engines
34	G-EASX	F308	0/10	Withdrawn from service April 1921
35	G-EASY	D4614	0/10	Withdrawn from service April 1921
36	G-EASZ	F310	0/11	Withdrawn from service April 1921
37	G-EATG	D4618	0/10	Withdrawn from service April 1921
38	G-EATH	D4631	0/10	Withdrawn from flying September 1923
39	G-EATJ	F307	0/10	Withdrawn from service April 1921
40	G-EATK	J2262	0/10	Jupiter IV engines 1921. Withdrawn late 1922
41	G-EATL	F312	0/10	Withdrawn from service April 1921
42	G-EATM	D4609	0/10	Withdrawn from service April 1921
43	G-EATN	J2261	0/10	Withdrawn from service spring 1922

NB: Individual fleet numbers 2-6, 8, 9, 17 and 29 relate to aircraft sold abroad.

Chapter 6

Emergency and makeshift bombers

IT MUST BE APPRECIATED that reconnaissance and bombing were the primary functions of both the Royal Naval Air Service and the Royal Flying Corps. Fighters were necessary for maintaining air superiority in order to permit other aircraft to attain the primary aims of the air arms.

Up to the beginning of 1917, it was not always possible to define the role of squadrons precisely. For example, a BE2c squadron, primarily concerned with reconnaissance and artillery spotting work, might be detailed to bomb a particular target for which some aircraft would carry a 112 lb bomb, but with no observer to compensate for the weight, while others would carry no bombs but pilot and gunner to act as escort—thereby fulfilling a fighter role.

As already related, the BE12 and Martinsyde Elephant, introduced as fighters, both functioned operationally mainly as bombers, and the Sopwith 1½ Strutter was built in two versions, single-seat bomber and two-seat fighter, both of which had bomb dropping capacity. Apart from these, many fighter aircraft, in squadrons that remained predominantly fighter units, functioned at times as bombers.

Sopwiths in the bombing role

Sopwith aircraft are often thought of as exclusively fighter aircraft, but several Sopwith fighter types were used as bombers. The Sopwith Camel was first used as a fighter bomber in September 1917 when the Camels of No 10 Squadron, RNAS, and No 70 Squadron, RFC, were fitted with racks under the fuselage to take four 20 lb bombs. The following month Sopwith Pups were being similarly used for night attacks on enemy airfields. When the new Sopwith fighter, the Dolphin, was introduced on the Western Front in the spring of 1918, its ability as a fighter could not be exploited as it was flung into battle to stem the German advance by strafing with machine-guns and bombs.

Two Sopwith types, the Rhino and Cobham, both triplanes, were designed specifically as bombers. The Rhino in 1917 was considered as a possible rival to the DH9 and it was similarly finished with grey-painted plywood forward and PC10 khaki-green doped fabric aft. An interesting marking facet of the two Rhino prototypes was their serial marking in the

'X'-series as X7 and X8. This denoted, in effect, that the aircraft had been originally built as a private venture; that is no official requirement existed for them when built. In 1917, to conserve raw materials at a time when German U-boats were a grave threat to Britain, it was made unlawful, under the Defence Regulations, to build aircraft except to official orders. However, special licence could be obtained by responsible organisations to build experimental aircraft and the granting of licences (numbered X for experimental) to Sopwith Aviation for the Rhinos resulted in this unusual prefix letter to such low numbers, outside the normal serial ranges. The later Cobham triplane bomber prototypes were built to a Ministry of Munitions specification, and so were numbered in the normal range as H671-673.

DH6—from trainer to bomber

A trainer that became a bomber in 1918 was the DH6, in rather the same way that in the later World War Tiger Moths were considered for fitting with bomb racks for maritime patrol. The swing to the Avro 504 series of aircraft for training made a surplus of DH6s available and, although not suited as bombers, the U-boats were such a menace that it was a case of trying anything that might restrict German submarine activity. A bomb of up to 100 lb could be carried by the DH6 used as a single-seater.

The aircraft had a battleship grey painted plywood finish forward and PC10 khaki-green doped fabric aft, in the same way as the other Aircraft Manufacturing Company products, DH4 and DH9. However, an unusual and exclusive marking feature of many DH6s was roundels marked on the upper-surface of the lower wing and under-surface of the upper wing in

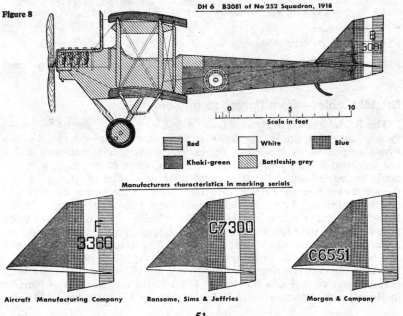

Figure 8

DH 6 B3081 of No 252 Squadron, 1918

Red   White   Blue

Khaki-green   Battleship grey

Scale in feet

Manufacturers characteristics in marking serials

Aircraft Manufacturing Company   Ransome, Sims & Jeffries   Morgan & Company addition to normal positions. This came about because the top and bottom wings, detachable from the wing centre-section, were identical in size and shape and so could be interchanged. In fact, they were issued to stores as left- or right-hand planes without the qualifying upper or lower of other biplane wings, and were finished with roundels on top and bottom surfaces.

Like DH4s and DH9s put out to contract, the particular manufacturer left a form of trademark in the way the serial number was marked—this was hardly ever on the rear fuselage, only occasionally on the fin, but usually on the rudder stripes.

The list of serials allotted to manufacturers is given in the Appendices; the list that follows is of particular DH6s that were distinguished operationally in a three-month period of 1918. A literal case of being mentioned in despatches:

Serial	Unit and base	Operational distinction
B2789	No 255 Sqn, Pembroke	Lt Nicholson dropped bomb on U-boat which failed to explode, August 24 1918
B3081	No 252 Sqn, Tynemouth	Pilot sighted U-boat's wake and dropped 100 lb bomb, August 17 1918
B3090	No 252 Sqn, Tynemouth	Pilot saw B3081 attack and tried to attract trawler to scene, August 17 1918
C2079	No 252 Sqn, Tynemouth	Pilot dropped bomb ten feet in front of U-boat, August 21 1918
C5172	No 256 Sqn, Seahouses	Flt Sgt Douglas sighted U-boat and dropped bomb, August 24 1918
C5207	No 250 Sqn, Padstow	Lt Shorter dropped two bombs on U-boat sighted, both of which failed to explode. Returned for more bombs, August 13 1918
C7336	No 526 Flt of No 256 Sqn, Haggerston	Capt Kennedy returning from escort duty at dusk sighted U-boat and bombed, September 11 1918
C9439	No 255 Sqn, Pembroke	Lt Peebles sighted periscope and bombed from 500 feet, 09.35 hrs, August 14 1918
F3349	No 255 Sqn, Pembroke	Joined C9439 in second attack, 11.00 hrs, August 14 1918
F3351	No 255 Sqn, Pembroke	Lt Peebles sighted periscope and bombed, August 24 1918

Bristol Fighter—from fighter to bomber

The Bristol Fighter was, as a famous test pilot said, a fighter by name, inclination and aptitude, yet the squadrons it equipped on the Western Front were officially classed as fighter reconnaissance squadrons—and it too was used for bombing. Up to 12 20-lb Cooper fragmentation bombs could be carried under the wings and these were used effectively against the advancing Germans on the Western Front in the spring of 1918 and on the retreating Turks in Palestine in the following autumn. These Bristols had the standard khaki-green PC10 finish of the period, but later, post-war, when their finish changed to silver, their bomb load was increased under their new role of army co-operation; first to one 112 lb high-explosive bomb and eight 20 lb Coopers, and later two 112 lb bombs.

Bristol Fighters remained in service until the 1930s and then for a brief period it was classed as a bomber in No 6 Squadron stationed at Ismailia in Egypt, with detachments in Palestine, during 1931. In April 1931, the

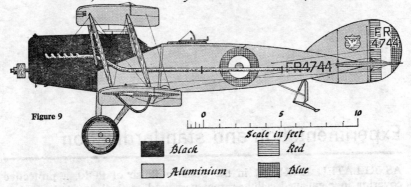

Bristol Fighter built as fighter 1918, used in army co-operation role in the twenties, shown when classified as bomber in No.6 Squadron, 1931.

Figure 9

Scale in feet

	Black		Red
	Aluminium		Blue

squadron's role was changed from army co-operation to bombing with planned replacement of the Bristol Fighters by Fairey Gordon day bombers. However, it was early 1931 before the Gordons arrived, so for nearly a year Bristol Fighters were officially bombers.

The unofficial No 6 Squadron marking (not until 1938 was a badge officially approved) of the period was an eagle with wings elevated. This eagle appeared as a white silhouette on a red shield on the fins of the aircraft, some of which were veterans of the First World War. Known squadron aircraft, built in 1918 and surviving until the 1930s, were F4744 and F4928, which were marked FR4744 and FR4928 to indicate that they had been completely rebuilt in the Middle East.

When the Gordons arrived early in 1932, the Bristol Fighter finally went out of first-line service in the RAF.

Chapter 7

Experimentation and standardisation

AS RELATED EARLIER in the book, a finish of PC10, a protective covering in pigmented cellulose that was used as final doping coat, was standard for all operational aircraft from mid-1916. Applied to upper and side surfaces it bestowed a shade officially described as khaki and alluded to variously as shades that ranged from green to brown. By November 16, a clear doped aircraft on the Western Front would have been sufficiently unusual to evoke a 'Make a note, Baring!' exclamation from General Trenchard. For, when on the 26th of that month Sopwith 1½ Strutter A1092 was delivered to France without its top plane having a PC10 coating, GHQ of RFC in the Field *were* sufficiently moved to complain. The Air Board replied in January 1917, that it had been reiterated to manufacturers that all machines were to be finished in 'a khaki colour'.

The Royal Naval Air Service also used PC10 together with PC12 which gave a browner finish. Similar instructions applied to naval contractors. These finishes were used irrespective of an aircraft's role and thereby embraced bombers; they remained standard until mid-1918 when experiments conducted in the winter of 1917 reached fruition.

Experiments in camouflage finishes were being conducted in four main directions:

(1) A new standard scheme to replace PC10/PC12 for all aircraft.
(2) A special camouflage for night flying aircraft.
(3) Special schemes to give minimum visibility to night-flying deep penetration aircraft viewed from below.
(4) Special schemes for low-flying observation, corps reconnaissance and ground strafing aircraft to give concealment from above.

The first three schemes, concerning bombers, are detailed below.

The new standard

PC10 was basically a protective covering by the inclusion of pigments in the cellulose used to dope the fabric of aircraft. Hitherto, a pigmented dope had been advocated only as a final finishing doping cover on top and side surfaces, with a protective transparent varnish in some cases. New schemes were devised in early 1918 to include pigments on all dope coatings and thereby improve the weathering properties, dispense with a final varnish and to be an overall finish.

The Royal Aircraft Establishment experimented with pigments in their Raftite dope and in October 1918 had two Handley Page 0/400 bombers, B8810 and B8811, finished in the new scheme and sent to No 5 Group, Dunkirk, for evaluation. To find how the dope weathered in sea air the Establishment asked the Isle of Grain experimental station to conduct experiments with a quantity of the new Raftite which they supplied.

At Grain, Armstrong Whitworth FK8s were allotted for the task; B4198 and F618 were each given new upper planes, fitted on October 5 and 18 1918 respectively, doped on *both* sides with the new mixture. The war was over by the time the weathering tests were over and the dope proven.

Meanwhile, industry had also been experimenting with similar schemes and in September 1918, PC10 and PC12 were officially superseded by an edict from the Ministry of Munitions advising manufacturers to adopt the new Armoid Scheme A, known as AMA, for all operational aircraft. The scheme was simple—three coats of pigmented dope which bestowed a finish similar to PC10.

The issue of the new dope was followed by a refinement into two types as follows:

AMAPD Khaki (Home and Western Front use);

AMAPDT Reddish brown (Tropical use).

(PD stood for protective dope and T for Tropical; the colours are the *official* descriptions.)

Thus from the end of 1918 camouflage colours were of two distinct standard shades, and in many cases were applied overall not merely to upper and side surfaces as before. Stocks of the new dope lasted until 1923.

Nivo for night

The new night camouflage was primarily a bomber scheme but extended to night fighters whose activity had resulted solely from the night bombing campaign. To commanders in the field, black had seemed the logical colour for aircraft operating at night and extra quantities of lampblack mixed in dope had bestowed a sooty appearance to many FE2bs at the Front. But the scientific staffs of the Ministry of Munitions, the 'boffins' of this earlier World War, were not convinced that black was the best colour for conceal-ment at night. On a very dark night this may well be so, but such condi-tions occasioned by a heavy overcast were unsuitable for air operations. Pilots and observers relied on stars for navigation and moonlight for locat-ing targets. Moonlight was reflected from land and sea, and in the half light, black would make an aircraft appear as a harsher silhouette than some other shades.

The problem of recommending the ideal was given to the Experimental Station, Orfordness, who were busily engaged on conducting armament experiments over ground currently being built upon and where many relics of those days have been recently unearthed by an RAF bomb disposal team. For their camouflage experiments of late 1917 the type of aircraft used is not known, but is presumed to be BE2cs, of which the station had several. One painted black and another in standard PC10 were the control batch for comparison with a third machine painted in various shades.

A pale blue finish proved something of a turning point. The aircraft in this finish appeared, according to the official report, to first come into visibility as a 'whitish ghost', whereas PC10, the khaki, had always appeared as a black silhouette. If these two shades represented the extremes of black and white, then somewhere between them, it was argued, would lie the shade that equalled 'night' and in theory render the aircraft invisible. But night itself, by virtue of the moon periods and the vagaries of the weather, was anything but standard. However, it was a pointer and a shade was devised, somewhere between the two, to give the best concealment in average night conditions.

The new shade was a mixture of yellow ochre, ultramarine blue and lithopone and the experimental staff claimed that as a night camouflage it would be difficult to improve upon. It was given the name Nivo and in effect gave fabric a greenish sheen. The Experimental Staff recommended it for all upper and side surfaces and in January 1918, a DH4 was finished in Nivo and sent to Farnborough for examination.

It took some six months to put Nivo dope into production and then only in small quantities to conduct service tests. Aircraft in the workshops at Hounslow and North Weald were given the new dope and their weathering was examined; finally, it was applied to 500 wing sets for Avro 504s under production. The finish was deemed proven in June 1918. From mid-1918 it was firmly established that all night flying machines should in future be in Nivo and day flying in khaki. Nivo became the styling for RAF night bombers until 1937.

But experiments were by no means at an end in 1918. The shade was decided but not the surface finish. The sheen of the glazed finish of Nivo was questioned and Orfordness started all over again to adjudge matt and glazed finishes; and the former was finally recommended.

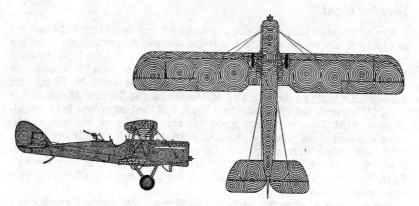

Figure 10: *A glimpse of the exotic: dazzle day scheme for DH9As evolved by C. F. Snowden Gamble, but too late in the war to be adopted.*

Day bomber schemes

Hitherto, the standard PC10 scheme had bestowed a camouflage colour for concealment from above. There was a need in 1917, with the expansion of bombing forces, for the high flying day bomber to have a camouflage rendering it difficult to observe from below. A special scheme had been

32 *An experimental mottled finish on a Handley Page 0/100 bomber. A report by the Orfordness Station stated, 'Provided that a few shades of say blue, green and brown, can be found, which would have the same power of reflecting moonlight as Nivo, there does seem some possibility in a mottled camouflage which would be as good as Nivo for night work and might prove useful for day work too'. As it was, the Handley Pages proved too vulnerable for day work* (via E. F. Cheesman).

33 *The first civil markings, carried by an 0/400, consisting of the official serial number marked large as a provisional civil registration. This machine later became G-5417, then G-EAAW* (J. M. Bruce/G. S. Leslie Collection).

34 *The original observation panel of the service 0/400 was the sole window space of the original Handley Page bombers converted for civil use. The fuel tanks, seen causing the hump under the top wing centre-section, were removed in all but the early civil conversions and replaced by tanks behind the engines, necessitating longer streamlined nacelles* (Real Photographs).

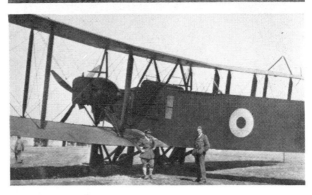

57

35 and 36   *F9569, a Mk II, the only Vimy to reach the Western Front and, below, Vimy IV H651 in PC10 finish (Imperial War Museum and Ministry of Defence).*

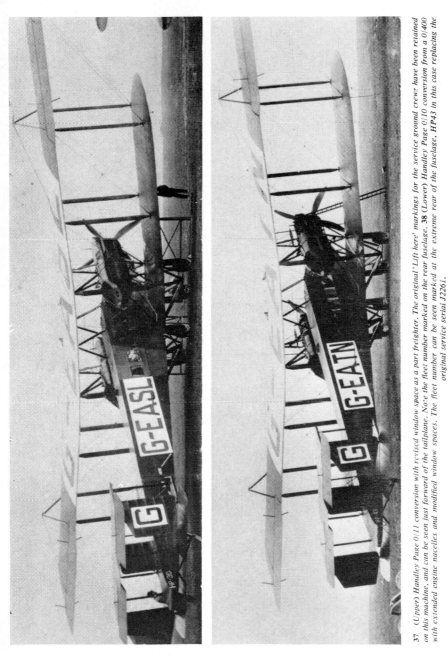

37 (Upper) Handley Page O/11 conversion with revised window space as a part freighter. The original 'Lift here' markings for the service ground crews have been retained on this machine, and can be seen just forward of the tailplane. Note the fleet number marked on the rear fuselage. 38 (Lower) Handley Page O/10 conversion from a O/400 with extended engine nacelles and modified window spaces. The fleet number can be seen marked at the extreme rear of the fuselage, HP43 in this case replacing the original service serial J2261.

39 *The Germans used printed fabrics of hexagons in six shades for their bombers as this captured AEG GIV shows. Fabric from captured examples was carefully examined by Ministry of Munitions' experts and reports were promulgated, but German methods did not influence British methods* (Imperial War Museum).

40 *DH4 A7459 with an RAF3A engine at Bacton in September 1917. Note special fawn and blue camouflage applied in connection with a project for a daylight bombing raid on Kiel* (J. M. Bruce/G. S. Leslie Collection).

41 *DH6 B2678 shows the peculiar result of standard wings for upper and lower fitting—roundels on all wing surfaces* (via J. T. C. Long).

42 *Martinsyde Elephant 7474, bombed up in the Middle East, seen with fuselage finished in PC10, but fin and wheel discs clear doped* (Ministry of Defence H1232).

tried with DH4s, as illustrated on page 60. Other schemes concerned a mottled finish and garish schemes designed to mislead gunners sighting on to the aircraft.

National markings

Roundels were unaffected by the new AMA standard dopings, except that, when it was applied overall, the lower as well as the upper wing roundels now had a one inch white surround.

In the new standard night scheme and experimental day schemes, roundels were radically affected. It was advocated that roundels be removed from upper wing surfaces and in late 1917 the Orfordness Station recommended the white inner be darkened. At this time, as will be evident from Chapter 1, an indication of nationality was an expedient, not as it became later, firstly through the medium of the League of Nations, and latterly through UNO, a matter of International Law.

Early in 1918, two BE2es had been sent to France for comparative tests; one had standard roundels and the other had one wing roundel placed further inboard than the other and the white replaced by cream. Nothing resulted until 11 days before the Armistice when, on November 1 1918, an order was promulgated throughout the RAF (formed April 1) to the effect that on all night-flying aircraft, the red centre of roundels would be increased to meet the blue outer and so eliminate the white.

The order did not reach many service units until after the Armistice. Some commanders, regarding it as a purely war-time measure, did not implement the change. However, it was later enforced on the production line for bombers and the red and blue roundel on a Nivo finish became the standard for night bombers lasting for almost the next 20 years.

Standardisation

In spite of the strictly official experimentation and recommendations by home establishments, semi-official experiments by individuals in the field with an inventive turn of mind and the views expressed by the aircraft industry, it was the local commander who had the final say.

Aircrew had, and evidence is that they still have, an inclination to embellish the aircraft they fly. Authority is often tolerant at first until such a stage is reached that instructions are issued that markings will be standardised.

It is thought that General Trenchard, during his tours along the front to find more bomber bases in August 1917, remarked on the unauthorised paintings on some aircraft; for on August 15 a Brigadier General, General Staff at RFC Advanced Headquarters in the Field, issued instructions that the GOC (General Officer Commanding Royal Flying Corps units on the Western Front) had decided that all British machines should be khaki (as indeed basically they all were) and that other markings would be restricted to:

a) National markings (ie, roundels);
b) The squadron marking on the fuselage;
c) The machine number on the rudder (ie, serial number);

D   61

d) The flight mark which could be either a single letter or a single number.

Like many instructions issued at high level, they did not take into account the facts of life of the man in the unit. Many aircraft were issued with the serial number on the fuselage because the rudder often needed replacement through heavy landings and the fuselage was the essential component that identified each aircraft. Similarly, how could a flight mark be limited to a single number when a bomber squadron had an establishment of 18 aircraft?

Evidently the GOC's views had been mildly intimated for the instruction explained that no repainting was to take place as a result of this decision. New machines brought on charge would conform to the new instructions and other aircraft on repainting for special reasons (for example after repair). The Brigadiers commanding the RFC Brigades in the Field were asked to aim at gradually eliminating the gaudy colours when it could be done without interfering with operational work. No officer could afford to disregard the wishes of the GOC, so that the general trend towards embellishing machines reached a peak on the Western Front in mid-August of 1917 and from that time gradually became more standardised.

Chapter 8

Wartime bombers in post-war service— DH10 and Vickers Vimy

OF SOME 20 DIFFERENT DESIGNS for twin-engined bombers in 1917-18, only two reached production status, the DH10 Amiens and Vickers FB27 Vimy; and while examples of both reached the Western Front in late 1918, neither type actually went on operations during the First World War. Large numbers of both types were surplus to requirements and plans to equip some Independent Air Force Squadrons with DH10s, and coastal patrol squadrons, commencing with No 274, with Vimys, were abandoned.

Contracts for over a thousand of each type were cancelled but well over a hundred of each had been fully erected when the cancellations were later effected. Placed in store, they were withdrawn in the immediate post-war years for squadron service. Their colours, therefore, were initially to the standards of 1918 and subsequently subject to the changes that came with a return to peacetime conditions.

These two types show a new trend in bombing colours—from the end of the First World War, colouring was apt to vary according to period of service, and to place of service.

From khaki to silver

Stocks of the AMA dopes became exhausted in 1923 and from this time new finishes were applied. These were APD and APDT for home and overseas use respectively; the A for (cellulose) acetate, PD for pigmented dope and T for tropical. With an aluminium covering the so-called 'silver' finish of RAF aircraft between the wars was bestowed. The effect of the tropical finish was the same as the home scheme, but the dope had different properties. This change showed a new philosophy in tropical finishes; hitherto the idea was to increase pigmentation to stop penetration of harmful sunrays, now it was to reflect, one might say deflect, these rays. And it looked good.

The range of pigments for colouring RAF aircraft at that time, with their official designations by name and code, was as follows:

Colour/name	Code	Pigments
Transparent	V114	Nil
Protective Covering	PC10	Yellow ochre and carbon black

Colour/name	Code	Pigments
Nivo	—	Yellow ochre, lithopone and ultramarine blue
Matt black	VB14	Carbon black
Protective Covering	PC12	Red iron oxide and carbon black
Aluminium Covering	V84	Aluminium powder
Red identification	VR3	Lithol red
White identification	VW3	Zinc oxide
Blue identification	VB2	Ultramarine blue and zinc oxide
Red* identification	VRN5	Red iron oxide
Blue* identification	VNB6	Ultramarine blue, zinc oxide and carbon black

* Identification colours for night-flying machines.

First of the bombers to be affected by the new finishes were the DH10 at the end of its service, and the Vimy at the start of its active service after, in many cases, several years in store. Both types were produced in several versions on which there is no straightforward serial marking guide.

DH10 Amiens

Ordered originally in late 1917 as a long-distance fighter for bombing escort work, the DH10 was finally ordered as a bomber in its Mk III version in early 1918.

Following the constructional methods employed by the Aircraft Manufacturing Company on the DH4 and DH9, the fuselage had plywood covering forward and fabric to the rear, except the tail-end, so that, as with its predecessors, there were areas of battleship grey and khaki for wood and fabric surfaces respectively. On the other hand, the wood on some was painted khaki to match the pigmented dope of the fabric.

Early production models had a khaki PC10 doping finish with plain under-surfaces and late production aircraft had khaki AMAPD overall. The DH10 entered squadron service post-war with No 97 Squadron in

Figure 11: *Detail view of a Liberty-engined DH10 which shows clearly the division of the doped fabric aft and the painted plywood forward on the fuselage.*

Figure 12: *Fore and aft views of a DH10 showing Scarff gun-rings with Lewis machine guns mounted. Partly obscured by the pilot's headrest fairing is the control column top which, like most twin- or multi-engined aircraft of the period, had a wheel control. Instruments on the dashboard were a compass, altimeter, air speed indicator, engine revolution counters and fuel pressure gauge.*

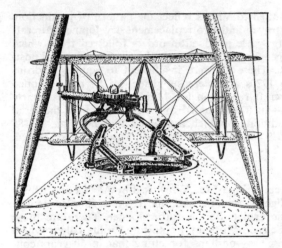

India and No 216 Squadron in Egypt; the former squadron was re-numbered No 60 on April 1 1920. Additionally, two DH10s were attached to No 27 Squadron in December 1922 for frontier operations. The aircraft used in these squadrons were shipped out, re-erected at depots, and given an AMAPDT reddish brown pigmented dope overall and plywood areas were painted to match. Only No 216 Squadron's DH10s appear to have been embellished. These had court card symbols on a white rectangular field each side of the nose.

A characteristic of initial DH10 markings was the particular manufacturers' styles; small batches emerged from each of the various contractors and those from the Aircraft Manufacturing Company and Mann, Egerton followed stylings set by earlier DH designs as illustrated in Chapter 4. The manufacturers were as tabled in the Appendices. Late in service, four DH10s survived to take on the new 'silver' finishes described for the Vimy.

Vickers Vimy

Vimy finishes followed the same trend as DH10 ones, initially with khaki doped fabric and grey on ply, then khaki AMA overall; but unlike the DH10, they did not appear in squadron service in drab finishes.

After the halting of deliveries to service at the end of 1918, plans were in hand for a limited number to serve in the Middle East and these were flown out in 1919. But as with Handley Page 0/400s (as related in Chapter 5), they had their share of accidents and F8622 crashed and burnt out en route near Lake Bracciano, Rome, on September 28 1919.

At home there was no immediate use for the Vimys envisaged and even three years later, in 1922, not one remained in squadron service; only 14 in training units were serviceable and the bulk, over 70, were in store. By 1924, plans for the post-war RAF were being effected and with the reactivating of Nos 9 and 58 Squadrons the Vimy entered squadron service. Meanwhile, others from store had been sent out East to bring Nos 45 and 216 Squadrons up to establishment. By this time silver finishes were in vogue.

The serial numbers allotted to Vimys reflect the pattern of production. Two prototypes were destroyed and two replacement development aircraft were ordered in lieu; large-scale production orders followed from which only a few aircraft emerged from five different plants; then the small post-war batches, totalling 30. These 30 were insufficient to equip squadrons and schools in the early 1920s and were supplemented by reconditioned earlier aircraft. Such aircraft rebuilt in the Middle East had this clearly indicated on the aircraft—an R was added to the index letter of the serial number. Thus, on reconditioning which amounted to rebuilding, F3185 became FR3185 and H5089 became HR5089. In all, 38 were reconditioned.

Transatlantic Vimy

The description of the colouring of the Vimy used by Alcock and Brown in their epic non-stop flight across the Atlantic is quite simple—neutral colour, no markings. The explanation is rather longer. There are those who, having visited the Science Museum, pontificate on the colour which they have seen for themselves—perhaps forgetting that in 50 years considerable re-painting has been necessary to keep the exhibit in a spruce condition.

Brown himself described the colour as grey. Photo tones show it must have been a light grey. This was probably the colour of the fabric itself which tended to become greyer for bombers as the war progressed, as the best quality Irish linen was not produced in sufficient quantities to meet the demands of such wide spreads. It was logical to use a clear dope since it was lighter than a pigmented dope—and weight was an important factor in view of the heavy fuel load.

Although Brown was still a serving officer, it was not an official RAF flight but a Vickers entry for the prize for the first crossing. Thus, RAF roundels or serial numbers were not applicable. It was technically a civil aircraft, but had been shipped to Newfoundland before the 1919 Air Navigation Directions regulating civil aviation were promulgated and therefore was not given a civil registration.

Chapter 9

The RAF's mainstay in the 1920s—DH9A

THE PROTRACTED SERVICE LIFE of the DH9A light day bomber reflects all the major changes in the colours and markings of day flying aircraft in the RAF from late in the First World War to the early 1930s.

It evolved like the most successful British bomber of the Second World War, the Lancaster, by the failure of an earlier type due to engine trouble. The DH9, with its BHP engine, could not match the early DH4 with its Rolls-Royce Eagle. Some attempt was made to substitute a 240 hp Fiat, but to effect the required improvement three possibilities were mooted in February 1918—to install a Napier Triple Four (named Lion the following month), to use the proven 350 hp Rolls-Royce Eagle VIII which was in great demand for other types, or to await the new 400 hp Liberty engine promised from America. Any of these measures, and all three were tried, necessitated an increase of 56 sq ft on wing area, and the new designation DH9A was applied to this feature, not the engine change.

The first Liberty-engined version, which became the standard, was airworthy from May 12 1918, when it was flown to Hendon for viewing by an American Commission. It was tested at Martlesham in June and placed in production.

General finish

As a follow-on from the DH9, re-engined and with larger wings, looking in fact much more like a DH4, the DH9A had all the initial marking characteristics of its two DH predecessors in the bombing role. Of similar construction, it had the forward and aft plywood-covered portions of the fuselage in battleship grey, and the fabric between and the wings in the khaki PC10.

It was logical that when the DH9A was put into large-scale production in 1918 that the earlier DH4/9 sub-contractors should tackle the new type. Thereby the characteristic styles of marking serials, shown in Chapter 4 for AMC, Westland and Mann, Egerton also apply to the DH9A.

The first squadron, No 110, did not arrive on the Western Front until August 31 1918 and, since from March 22 distinguishing squadron markings had been banned on all but fighter units for security reasons, individual letters or numbers were the only marking. An exception was No 110's

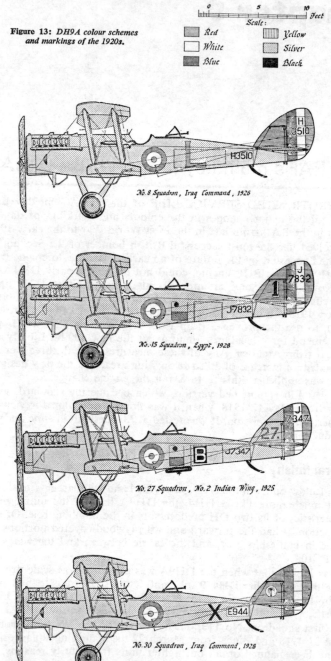

Figure 13: *DH9A colour schemes and markings of the 1920s.*

Scale:

Red	Yellow
White	Silver
Blue	Black

No. 8 Squadron, Iraq Command, 1926

No. 15 Squadron, Egypt, 1928

No. 27 Squadron, No. 2 Indian Wing, 1925

No. 30 Squadron, Iraq Command, 1928

THE DH9A

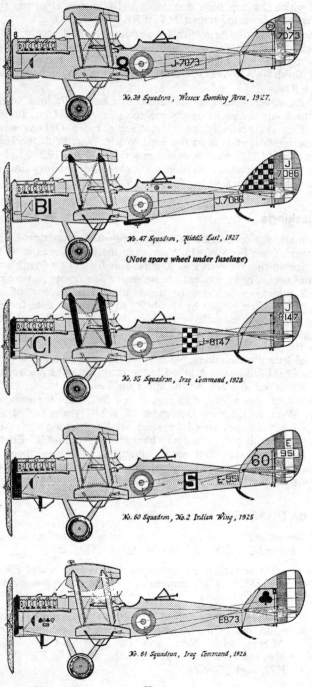

No. 39 Squadron, Wessex Bombing Area, 1927.

No. 47 Squadron, Middle East, 1927

(Note spare wheel under fuselage)

No. 55 Squadron, Iraq Command, 1928

No. 60 Squadron, No. 2 Indian Wing, 1925

No. 84 Squadron, Iraq Command, 1925

aircraft which, having been donated by His Serene Highness the Nizam of Hyderabad, bore the names HYDERABAD 1, 2, 3, etc.

By the time of the Armistice four squadrons had received the DH9A which was chosen as the only light bomber type to equip the peacetime force. From the early 1920s it appeared at first in the reddish brown tropical finish — AMAPDT which bestowed a shade best described as Vandyke Red.

Soon the silver shades, as described in Chapter 7, took over and the DH9A took up duties in peacetime roles in Aden, Iraq, India and the Middle East. Surprisingly, as it may seem, more DH9As were lost in peacetime operations than in the First World War. With the Independent Air Force in 1918, 21 were wrecked in service; in the 1920-23 phase of the Iraq operations alone, 11 were lost in rebel-held territory and a total of 57 were put out of action temporarily by ground fire.

Unit markings

Most markings on bomber aircraft were purely functional. During the later stages of the First World War, when the DH9A was entering squadron service on the Western Front, close-knit formation flying was becoming a vital necessity to concentrate defensive fire from the rear gunners to ward off attacking fighters. In peacetime the efficiency of a bomber squadron was often judged by its ability to fly immaculate formations. In forming up it was essential each pilot knew his place and since serial markings were a standard 8-inch letter/numeral size they were not large enough for individual identity to be ascertained easily. Thus the large individual letters or numbers, placed mid-fuselage or on noses in white on war-time khaki finishes, continued in the reconstituted squadrons in peacetime, but marked in black on the silver finishes.

Then colour was added, and regularised following the issue of an Air Ministry Weekly Order on December 18 1924. This specified that distinguishing flight colours could be used at the discretion of Air Officers Commanding, with red, yellow and blue for 'A', 'B' and 'C' Flights respectively. The result was that some squadrons displayed their individual letters in flight colours and these colours were also used, in certain squadrons, for marking the rudders and/or tailplanes of flight leaders' aircraft.

Notes on DH9As in service units

No 3 Squadron: Special three-seat version used, in silver finish, 1920-21, examples being H3512, H3515, H3518, H3539, H3540.

No 8 Squadron: Individual letters used. Both E886 and E8669 as 'O', and E914 and H3525 as 'P', emphasise the rate of replacement necessary in desert areas.

No 27 Squadron: Sharing the aerodrome at Risalpur with No 60 Squadron in the mid-1920s, the two squadrons ran a combined scheme of letters A to M reserved for No 27 and N to Z for No 60, each displayed in a panel as illustrated on page 68. Examples are 'A' E828, 'B' J7347, 'C' E9948, 'D' H72, and 'E' 8673.

THE DH9A

No 30 Squadron: Operating over the desert wastes of Iraq, the squadron instituted orange upper-surface wingtips to assist searchers in the event of forced landings. In the mid-1920s the squadron used individual symbols on the fin in lieu of letters or numerals, eg E802 had a six-point star and J7124 a swastika. These symbols were repeated on the upper-surface of the top wing centre-section.

No 39 Squadron: Individual numerals used, displayed by the fuselage roundel, eg, '7' E960, '8' J7073, '9' E8695. The squadron number was displayed in small figures in a circle on the fin as drawn on page 69.

No 45 Squadron: Individual numerals displayed on fins, and repeated on upper-surface of top wing centre-section.

No 47 Squadron: In the mid-1920s the individual markings adopted were Roman or Arabic numerals I-VI (or 1-6) on nose prefixed by flight letter. Chequered tail markings were in black and the flight colour appropriate. At one stage aircraft bore individual names marked on the nose, eg, E850 PERSEUS, H3635 DARIUS and JR7007 NIOBE.

No 55 Squadron: In the mid-1920s a squadron marking of a chequered band around the fuselage was in vogue using black with the appropriate flight colour. These colours were repeated on the radiator shutters. Individual markings on the nose were similar to No 47 Squadron, the CO's aircraft being the exception with the squadron number in place of the flight letter and individual number. Examples were 'CI' E8796, later J8147, 'CII' E8806, and 'CIII' F2778. The Commanding Officer's aircraft bore the squadron number '55' on the nose; in 1928 this was J8102.

No 60 Squadron: See No 27 Squadron. Examples are 'W' J7341 and 'X' H3626.

No 84 Squadron: Symbols used in lieu of letters or numerals for individual markings, eg, E849 bore a swastika on the nose.

No 99 Squadron: Wartime khaki/grey finishes; F967, F1035 and F2739 were used late 1918/early 1919.

No 207 Squadron: In 1922 when sent to Constantinople, E852, E871, F1616, H138, J556, J557 and J561 were drawn from the Ascot Depot in silver finish and used without embellishment. Re-established in the UK later, individual markings 1 to 6 prefixed by the flight letter were marked on the nose of aircraft, eg, No 4 of 'C' Flight, 'C4', was E8805. Radiator shutters were chequered in black and the standard flight colour.

No 600 (City of London) Squadron: Squadron crest on nose and '600' marked large on the fuselage side were applied among others to J8165, J8223 and J8502. Individual letters were marked on the fuselage side between the wings, J8223 being 'C'.

No 601 (County of London) Squadron: In the County's case, the squadron number was marked on the nose in the flight colour and the squadron badge aft of the roundel. Squadron aircraft were E8605, E8627, J8108, J8114, J8130, J8161, J8224 and J8428.

RAF Training Mission, Russia: E9751, F1089, F1094, etc, in standard wartime finish, 1919.

Serial numbers

The range of numbers used are tabled in the Appendices. They were all original aircraft up to J6000. From J7008 they were built up from wartime production contract aircraft which had been dismantled and stored, or incompleted airframes. Many more were in turn re-built again and those reconditioned overseas had an 'R' added to the serial prefix letter, eg, JR7842 and JR7808.

While the serial number gives a trace of individual identity, the linking of a machine with a particular unit can only be taken as at a particular time, eg J8472 served in Nos 600, 603 and 604 Squadrons, in turn, during a single year.

Some twenty DH9As served with the United States Marine Corps in France during November 1918. They bore USMC numbers E1, E2, E3, et seq, being ex-E8465, E8477, E8466, etc, respectively.

Chapter 10

The Vickers bomber transports—Vernon, Victoria and Valentia

THE SUCCESS OF THE VIMY was exploited by a commercial version with a large, almost bulbous, front fuselage. Forty were supplied to China, one to Russia and five were built for the Royal Air Force as Vimy ambulances.

The post-war policy of substituting military forces in Iraq by air patrols, together with commitments in the Near East, led to a new type of RAF aircraft that reached its hey-day in the years between the wars, the bomber transport. This type of aircraft had to be capable of transporting troops to trouble-spots and be able to engage in punitive bombing attacks on the bases of recalcitrant tribesmen. A crew of three was normal and 11 passengers could be carried in the first version, which was increased to 23 later in the Vickers bomber-transport series.

Vickers received an order for 30 Vernon transports fitted with Rolls-Royce Eagle engines, but the last ten of these, and all subsequent, were to a new standard with Napier Lion engines. Their construction conditioned their finish.The fore-part of the fuselage in Consuta copper-sewn plywood was coated with aluminium paint initially and sometimes in grey in service. The rest of the fuselage and wings were fabric covered. Stretched tightly over the fuselage and wings, it showed clearly the run of longerons and the positions of ribs.

Doping was a major and tedious process. It was specified to take place in a dry shop at a constant temperature of 70° with the air being changed 30 times an hour. The first coat of tightening dope had to be brushed well in, to ensure penetration of the weft and warp of the fabric. Four evenly spread coats of the same dope had to follow at set intervals to allow one coat to dry before the next was applied. Being colourless the aircraft appeared the slightly off-white of the Irish linen. Next came the colouring dope, PC12, containing powdered aluminium to give the silver finish typical of the period. In rather the same way that blood is a yellow liquid that appears red from the colour of the corpuscles floating in it, so the dope was a colourless liquid with millions of particles of aluminium. It had to be stirred well before using, and at frequent intervals during use, to ensure an overall even silvery effect.

This silver finish, pleasing to the eye, was purely functional. For an aircraft destined for the tropics a heat-reflecting surface was essential to reduce cabin heat. To protect this finish, a final coat of varnish known as

(A) Squadron marking on No 45 Squadron Vernons

(B) Squadron marking on No 70 Squadron Victorias

(C) Squadron marking on No 216 Squadron Valentias

Figure 14

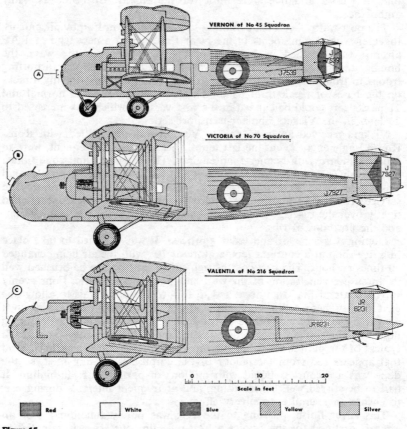

VERNON of No 45 Squadron

VICTORIA of No 70 Squadron

VALENTIA of No 216 Squadron

0   10   20
Scale in feet

Red   White   Blue   Yellow   Silver

Figure 15

V84 was applied which added to the reflecting properties as well as acting as a protective cover.

Roundels, marked at the tip of the wings of Vernons, were 10 feet 6 inches in diameter and thereby some of the largest ever to appear on British aeroplanes.

The Vernon went into service with two squadrons, Nos 45 and 70, both based in the Middle East and, although used mainly for transport duties, both were classed as bomber squadrons. These squadrons introduced individual names for their aircraft; a practice that persists to today with RAF transport aircraft. In No 70 Squadron names such as *Vagabond*, *Valkyrie* and *Venus* adorned their Vernons.

To replace the Vernon, Vickers produced the Victoria, which departed from the original Vimy's form, by wings of increased span, a much longer fuselage and a completely re-designed tail unit. It replaced Vernons in No 70 Squadron in the Middle East, equipped No 216 Squadron in the same regions and was used by the Bomber Transport Flight in India.

Still classed as bomber transports, their active operations in the troubled territories of the Middle East and India were largely confined to trans-porting roles. During the 1928-29 riots in Kabul, the capital of Afghanistan, when the British subjects were endangered, they evacuated the majority of the 586 civilians in the world's first major airlift.

Apart from their potential dual role of bomber transports, they were at times bomber transporters, flying-in reserves of fuel, ammunition and bombs to squadrons engaged on operations in frontier regions.

For the tropics, aluminium remained their appropriate overall finish. Roundels were marked large as on the Vernons. Serials in standard black 8-inch characters were marked across the rudder stripes and in 4-foot characters under the wings. Since neither were clearly discernible to pilots flying in level formation, distinguishing individual letters were often marked on the side of the nose.

Victorias were produced in several small batches spanning both the 'J' and 'K' serial prefix ranges. These batches resulted from replacement requirements for, although the Victorias were sturdy aircraft, pioneering Imperial Airways routes across the Middle East, there was a series of unfortunate accidents in No 70 Squadron in 1928. First, J8229 caught fire on the ground and was destroyed on April 21. Next month a gale destroyed J7924 and the following month, on June 7, due to petrol cock not being turned off, fuel caught fire and wrecked J7923, J7927, J8226 and J8227 that were parked close together. Before the year was out J8915 had also gone up in smoke in a refuelling accident. On the other hand, in the air the aircraft had a wonderful safety record, each averaging over 2,000 flying hours.

Progressive uprating of Lion engines and the introduction of more metal parts in the airframe (wood warped badly in tropical climates) led to successive marks of Victorias and a re-engining to Bristol Pegasus engines together with other refinements brought about a re-naming as the Valentia. Many Victorias were converted to Valentias and new orders for Valentias were placed.

Such was the shortage of transport aircraft in the Middle East, that Valentias were kept in service until 1944 and during the Second World

War, in desert camouflage, actually operated on bombing missions including over Sidi Barrani in the Western Desert Campaign and over Rutbah Wells during the Iraqi Insurrection.

The service of Vernons, Victorias and Valentias spanned all the major changes in markings, which are reiterated here:

From March 1927 serials marked large in black under the wings;

From August 1930 to October 1930 order of rudder stripes reversed to red leading and blue trailing;

From August 1934 rudder striping discontinued altogether and roundels on wings reduced in size in order not to overlap into ailerons.

On Valentias the fuselage roundels were changed to the red and blue 'B' Type when war was declared in September 1939 and given a local camouflage, replaced by a standard desert scheme later. Some already had defensive armament from modification carried out in 1936 in the Abyssinia crisis. This consisted of Scarff gun rings mounting Lewis guns in the nose and mid-fuselage positions.

Vickers bomber-transport versions

Type and mark	Engines (×2)	Vickers Type No	Remarks concerning changes
Vernon I	360 hp R-R Eagle VIII	—	Initial production
Vernon II	450 hp Napier Lion II	—	Engine change
Vernon III	450 hp Napier Lion III	—	Uprated engines, extra fuel
Victoria I	450 hp Napier Lion IA	56	Prototype
Victoria II	450 hp Napier Lion II	81	2nd Prototype
Victoria III	450 hp Napier Lion II	117	Initial production
Victoria IIIA	450 hp Napier Lion II	138	Metal wings introduced
Victoria IV	450 hp Napier Lion II/V	158	Metal-framed version
Victoria IV	450 hp Bristol Jupiter III	145	Engine change, J9250 only
Victoria V	550 hp Napier Lion XI	169	Uprated Lion engines
Victoria V	440 hp Bristol Jupiter XFB	241	K2340 engine test bed
Victoria V	555 hp Bristol Pegasus IM3	248	K2340 and K2808 test beds
Victoria V	550 hp Napier Lion XI	261/274	K2344 for blind flying
Victoria V	550 hp Napier Lion XI	274	K2344 modified
Victoria V	575 hp Bristol Pegasus IIL3	260	K2807 re-engined to Mk VI
Victoria VI	575 hp Bristol Pegasus IIL3	262	Mk VI production
Valentia I	575 hp Bristol Pegasus IIM3	276	Tropical trials
Valentia I	575 hp Bristol Pegasus IIM3	278	K2344 re-engined
Valentia I	575 hp Bristol Pegasus IIM3	282	K4632 with loud-hailer
Valentia I	575 hp Bristol Pegasus IIM3	283	K4633 armament experiments

Victoria-Valentia production/conversion list

Serial, type and conversions	Remarks on service or disposal
J6860 Victoria I (Prototype)	First flew August 22 1922
J6861 Victoria II (Prototype)	First flew January 1923
J7921 Victoria III-IV—Valentia	Served in 70 Sqn as Valentia
J7922 Victoria III	70 Sqn. Destroyed by fire, January 7 1928
J7923 Victoria III	70 Sqn. Destroyed in gale, May 22 1928
J7924 Victoria III	Served in Middle East, 70 Sqn
J7925 Victoria III	
J7926 Victoria III	
J7927 Victoria III	70 Sqn. Destroyed by fire, June 7 1928

43 *The laborious, but usual way of marking up roundels in the First World War. During 1918 experiments were conducted in producing printed fabrics of identification markings to stick on fuselage sides. A specification was approved by September that year, but the cessation of hostilities halted the production of these fabrics* (Imperial War Museum Q 34010).

44 *As early as June 1918, the American aircraft assembly organisation adopted Nivo as their standard for the finish of night bombers. Here a V/1500 is being erected at Ford Junction, October 24 1918, for training American crews* (via D. A. S. McKay).

45 *HMA* Silver Star *of the 86th (Communications) Wing showing the increased window size. The fuselage band (in this case partly obscured by the interplane struts) of red/blue/red/blue/red was a characteristic of aircraft of the 86th Wing* (Ministry of Defence H1858).

46 *Standard factory finish of a DH9A built by Mann, Egerton & Company of Norwich.*

47 *DH9A in North Russia. 1919, showing all the factory-finish characteristics of the Aircraft Manufacturing Company.*

48 *Blood-red DH9A used by Air Vice-Marshal H. Brooke-Popham when Air Officer Commanding Iraq Command, 1929 (Ministry of Defence H1045).*

49 *Depot DH9A at Karachi, 1929, in standard aluminium finish of the period.*

50 *Standard finish of newly built DH10s, in khaki-brown fabric with battleship-grey ply at both ends of fuselage, is shown in port and starboard views (see photo 51) of E5557, a DH10C (Rolls-Royce Eagle engines).*

51 *The marking of the serial on only the red and white stripes of the rudder is an exclusive characteristic of aircraft built by the Aircraft Manufacturing Company (G. S. Leslie/J. M. Bruce Collection).*

52 *E5507 survived to the days of an overall 'silver' finish with its serial repainted in standard styling (G S. Leslie/J. M. Bruce Collection).*

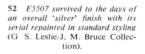

53 *DH9A H3627 of No 55 Squadron showing that squadron marking styles came in just before khaki finishes went out (Ministry of Defence H1537).*

54 *(Top left) Fairey Fox in standard finish.* 55 *(Above) Avro Aldershot in standard finish of the type, with black cowlings.* 56 *(Left) Fairey Fawn of No 12 Squadron showing the circular squadron motif on the fin* (Ministry of Defence H573).

Serial, type and conversions	Remarks on service or disposal
J7928 Victoria III	216 Sqn. Used in long-range flights, 1926
J7929 Victoria III	216 Sqn. Used in long-range flights, 1926
J7930 Victoria III	Served in 216 Sqn
J7931 Victoria III	Served in 216 Sqn
J7932 Victoria III	216 Sqn. Rebuilt as JR7932
J7933 Victoria III	Used in propeller and engine trials
J7934 Victoria III-IV	
J7935 Victoria III-IV	58 Sqn, 1926. Middle East, 1929. Crashed May 17 1935
J8061 Victoria IIIA	First of batch ordered May 1926
J8062 Victoria IIIA-V-VI—Valentia	216 Sqn. Burnt out on ground, September 19 1942
J8063 Victoria IIIA-V—Valentia	216 Sqn. Rebuilt as JR8063
J8064 Victoria IIIA	
J8065 Victoria IIIA-VI—Valentia	Withdrawn December 1937 after 3,222 hours flying
J8066 Victoria IIIA	
J8226 Victoria IIIA	70 Sqn. Wrecked by fire, June 7 1928
J8227 Victoria IIIA	70 Sqn. Wrecked by fire, June 7 1928
J8228 Victoria IIIA	
J8229 Victoria IIIA	70 Sqn. Wrecked by fire, April 21 1928
J8230 Victoria IIIA-V—Valentia	216 Sqn. Wrecked, November 19 1937
J8231 Victoria IIIA-V-VI—Valentia	216 Sqn. Sold to Indian Government
J8232 Victoria IIIA-VI—Valentia	Sold to Indian Government
J8233 Victoria IIIA	
J8234 Victoria IIIA	
J8235 Victoria IIIA	
J8915 Victoria IIIA	Wrecked by fire, September 25 1928
J8916 Victoria IIIA-IV-VI—Valentia	70 Sqn. Withdrawn, February 4 1937
J8917 Victoria IIIA-IV	
J8918 Victoria IIIA-IV	
J8919 Victoria IIIA-IV—Valentia	70 Sqn. Beyond repair, July 6 1938
J8920 Victoria IIIA-IV-V-VI	216 Sqn. Wrecked, 1931, and rebuilt as JR8920
J8921 Victoria IIIA-IV-VI—Valentia	70 Sqn. Sold to South Africa, September 1940
J8922 Victoria IIIA-IV-VI	216 Sqn. Crashed, February 10 1937
J8923 Victoria IIIA	
J8924 Victoria IIIA-IV	
J8925 Victoria IIIA-IV-VI	
J8926 Victoria IIIA-IV-V-VI	216 Sqn. Crashed, July 9 1937
J8927 Victoria IIIA	
J8928 Victoria IIIA	
J8929 Victoria IIIA	
J9250 Victoria IV	Trials aircraft. Crashed, March 29 1931
J9760 Victoria IV-V-VI—Valentia	First of batch ordered October 1929
J9761 Victoria IV-V	
J9762 Victoria IV-VI—Valentia	Served in 70 Sqn
J9763 Victoria IV-V-VI	70 Sqn. Crashed, October 11 1935 in Iraq
J9764 Victoria IV-V—Valentia	Experimentally fitted with Italian engines
J9765 Victoria IV-V-VI—Valentia	Rebuilt as JR9765
J9766 Victoria IV-V-Valentia	Served in No 70 Sqn
K1310 Victoria V	First of batch ordered April 1930
K1311 Victoria V-VI—Valentia	'B' of 70 Sqn
K1312 Victoria V-VI—Valentia	Converted to Valentia, April 1936
K1313 Victoria V—Valentia	216 Sqn. Rebuilt as KR1313
K1314 Victoria V-VI—Valentia	Sold to South Africa
K1315 Victoria V-VI	216 Sqn. Crashed, November 19 1935
K2340 Victoria V-VI—Valentia	Trials aircraft. Served in 31 Sqn
K2341 Victoria V—Valentia	Served in 216 Sqn
K2342 Victoria V-VI—Valentia	Served in Middle East and India
K2343 Victoria V-VI—Valentia	Disposal on June 2 1937

Serial, type and conversions	Remarks on service or disposal
K2344 Victoria V—Valentia	Used at Central Flying School
K2345 Victoria V—Valentia	Fitted with public address system
K2791 Victoria V—Valentia	Disposal on January 24 1934
K2792 Victoria V—Valentia	Rebuilt as KR2792
K2793 Victoria V—Valentia	70 Sqn. Rebuilt as KR2793
K2794 Victoria V—Valentia	Crashed, November 9 1936
K2795 Victoria V—Valentia	Disposal on January 22 1941
K2796 Victoria V—Valentia	Sold to South Africa
K2797 Victoria V—Valentia	Disposal in August 1940
K2798 Victoria V-VI—Valentia	Disposal in July 1941
K2799 Victoria V—Valentia	Served in Iraq, 1940
K2800 Victoria V—Valentia	70 Sqn. Sold to South Africa
K2801 Victoria V—Valentia	Sold to South Africa
K2802 Victoria V—Valentia	Sold to South Africa
K2803 Victoria V—Valentia	Disposal on March 31 1943
K2804 Victoria V—Valentia	Sold to South Africa
K2805 Victoria V—Valentia	Sold to South Africa
K2806 Victoria V-VI—Valentia	Disposal in October 1939
K2807 Victoria V-VI—Valentia	Used in engine-carrying trials
K2808 Victoria V-VI—Valentia	Used by Comm Flight Habbaniya, 1941
K3159 Victoria VI—Valentia	First production Mk VI
K3160 Victoria VI—Valentia	Served in Iraq and Middle East to 1940
K3161 Victoria VI—Valentia	Disposal on November 9 1940
K3162 Victoria VI—Valentia	Rebuilt as KR3162
K3163 Victoria VI—Valentia	216 Sqn. Rebuilt as KR3163
K3164 Victoria VI—Valentia	Disposal in October 1939
K3165 Victoria VI—Valentia	Disposal in October 1939
K3166 Victoria VI—Valentia	216 Sqn. Crashed, July 7 1937
K3167 Victoria VI—Valentia	Disposal on October 7 1941
K3168 Victoria VI—Valentia	'K' of 70 Sqn as Valentia
K3169 Victoria VI—Valentia	Sold to India
K3599 Valentia	Served in 70 Sqn
K3600 Valentia	Sold to India
K3601 Valentia	Used at Cranwell. Crashed, February 4 1941
K3602 Valentia	Served in Middle East
K3603 Valentia	'Flying Classroom' conversion
K3604 Valentia	Disposal on March 6 1941
K3605 Valentia	'O' of 216 Sqn
K3606 Valentia	Disposal in October 1939
K3607 Valentia	'P' of 216 Sqn
K3608 Valentia	Serving in Iraq, 1941
K3609 Valentia	Missing on flight in India, May 6 1941
K3610 Valentia	Disposal on May 6 1951
K3611 Valentia	Lost by enemy action, August 25 1941
K3612 Valentia	'F' of 216 Sqn
K3613 Valentia	Served in 70 Sqn
K3614 Valentia	Served in 70 Sqn
K4630 Valentia	Disposal in March 1947
K4631 Valentia	Sold to South Africa
K4632 Valentia	Fitted with loud-hailing equipment
K4633 Valentia	Gun position trials aircraft
K4634 Valentia	Served in India
K4635 Valentia	Disposal in India, March 16 1940
K5605 Valentia	Disposal on November 22 1940
K8848 Valentia	Disposal in September 1941
K8849 Valentia	Disposal on April 22 1941
K8850 Valentia	Used by Electrical and Wireless School, Cranwell
K8851 Valentia	Sold to South Africa
K8852 Valentia	Disposal on July 6 1941

Chapter II

Post-war single-engined bombers

IN THE EARLY and mid-1920s, marking regulations made no distinction between fighters and bombers; the differences concerned whether an aeroplane had a day flying or night flying role. However, no successful night fighter had then reached service, so both RAF schemes were applied to bombers and only the day scheme to fighters. These were aluminium pigmented dope or paints giving a silver appearance for day roles and Nivo giving a dull green for night roles.

At this time only the single-engined bombers had speed sufficient to be classed as day bombers, while the lumbering weight-lifting, twin-engined bombers were all night bombers, so in effect the two RAF finishes were applied to bombers according to their configuration. In this chapter the day bomber element is surveyed.

Avro Aldershot

With a span only an inch less than that of a Vimy, the Aldershot, classed as a medium bomber, was an extremely large aircraft for a single-engined aeroplane. The fabric covering the metal structure was ADP doped giving a silver appearance. To match this, the ply-covered forward-fuselage decking and metal cowling were similarly painted, but such was the glare to the crew, that black was soon substituted on this area.

Two prototypes, J6852 and J6853, were followed by 15 production aircraft, J6942-6956, from which were drawn the aircraft to equip the only Aldershot squadron, No 99, established on a twin-flight basis at Bircham Newton, 1924-26.

In squadron service individual identity, apart from the small display of their serial numbers, was by large white numerals on the engine cowling. Examples are shown in the drawing on page 84, plus '4' J6956 and '8' J6944.

Fairey Fawn

It was envisaged that the Fawn would replace the DH9A but, for financial reasons, it was outlived by its predecessor. Fawns were finished conventionally, silver overall with a highly polished, natural metal, engine cowling.

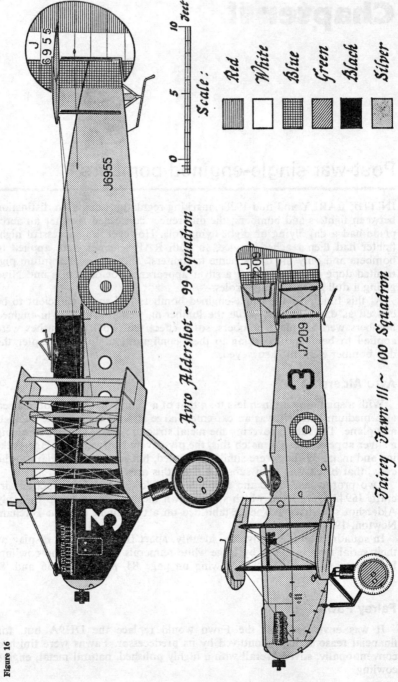

Figure 16

Scale:

Red
White
Blue
Green
Black
Silver

Avro Aldershot ~ 99 Squadron

Fairey Fawn III ~ 100 Squadron

A characteristic of Fairey aircraft was a visible constructor's number placed in small stencilling adjacent to the serial number on the rear fuselage. In service it was sometimes painted out, but invariably it was marked on initial delivery. Official Fawn serial numbers were all in the 'J' series and all Fairey numbers were prefixed 'F'—they still are and recently reached up to F9731 for Wasp HAS1 XV636 built at the Hayes Division of Westland Helicopters, once Fairey Aviation works. Matching J/F numbers for Fawns were:

Serial number	Fairey number
J6907	F403
J6908-6909	F404-405
J6990-6991	F415-416
J7182-7231	F481-530
J7768-7779	F783-794
J7978-7985	F865-872

The Fawn equipped three first-line squadrons, Nos 11, 12 and 100, all on a three-flight basis. Of these, No 12 Squadron used a small motif, in the manner of No 39 Squadron's DH9As shown in Chapter 9, as a squadron marking; but No 100 Squadron, shortly before discarding its Fawns, set a style for home-based bomber squadrons, that of marking its squadron number on the fuselage side.

Cubaroo

Among the experimental bombers of the 1920s was the Blackburn T4 Cubaroo, one of the largest single-engined bombers ever built. Powered by a 1,000 hp Napier Cub which had been tried in the Aldershot Mk II, the Cubaroo's wings spanned 88 feet. It was designed as a torpedo-bomber with a 3½-ton useful load, including a 1½-ton torpedo or bombs in lieu.

Bearing an aluminium cover, the two Cubaroos built were numbered N166 and N167 in the series reserved for prototypes with a naval or coastal application. Its Avro counterpart, the twin-Condor-engined Ava, was similarly finished with the serials N171 and N172 for Mks I and II respectively.

The experimentals

Among the experimental bombers that appeared in the 1920s was one by Gloster, a firm specialising almost exclusively in fighters. Their Goral, although usually described as a general purpose aircraft, was considered by the Air Ministry as a bomber in 1927. This aircraft utilised DH9A wings but only the one, J8678, was built. Finished with an aluminium covering, it was one of the first of the 'silver' aircraft to have a black decking to reduce glare for pilot and rear gunner.

An earlier contender for 26/23, the main single-engined bomber specification of the mid-1920s, was the Bristol Berkeley of which three, J7403-7405, were built. A decision not to consider single-engined aircraft for night bombing precluded the possibility of a production order and the Handley Page Handcross (three built, J7498-7500) and Westland Yeovil (three built, J7508-7510) were similarly shelved, leaving only the Horsley in the field as both torpedo bomber and day bomber. The serial numbers borne by these and other experimental bombers are included in the Appendices.

Chapter 12

The Virginia night bombers—Mks I to X

THE MOST FAMOUS of the RAF night bombers between the wars, but essentially a home-based aircraft, the Virginia entered service in 1923, and formed the sole equipment of three first-line bombing squadrons (Nos 7, 9 and 58) from the mid-1920s to mid-1930s, and of a fourth (No 10) from 1932-34. It also formed the main equipment of two Special Reserve squadrons (Nos 500 and 502) in the 1930s and, for a period in the later 1930s, partially provided the interim equipment of four newly re-formed regular squadrons (Nos 51, 97, 214 and 215).

Overall finishes

While the Virginia will always be associated with the Nivo (dull green) finish of night bombers between the wars its long years of service spanned finishes from the silver (aluminium pigment) to the camouflage patterns of the Second World War. The distinctions can be made quite clearly. Up to and including J7275, the tenth Virginia built, all were in silver finish with standard roundels of red, white and blue. In this finish they first entered service with No 7 Squadron. From J7418, the 11th built, all were delivered in Nivo, the finish that gave a dark green appearance, with night roundels of red inners and blue outers—white being excluded.

However, by 1927, all Virginias were in Nivo finish. Early deliveries were recalled to the works for modification to later standards and were re-doped Nivo after conversion. Virginias up to J8914 were constantly being withdrawn for modification and the table on page 90 shows the standard by Mark number to which built and the subsequent conversions of each airframe. Some of the Marks refer to changes in rigging and the progressive replacement of wooden structural members by metal parts; the most important change visually was at the Mk VII, introducing a sweep-back on the wings and revising the nose, giving a blunter appearance, and the Mk IX introducing a rear turret among other changes. After J8914 all were produced as Mark Xs.

This big biplane bomber actually saw service in the Second World War. When war was declared in 1939, four were still in service. The oldest was J7130 used at Farnborough for parachute experiments. Nivo finish had been considered a sufficient camouflage in the late 1930s when other aircraft were given the disruptive pattern of dark earth and dark green, but by 1939 Nivo was not being stocked and Virginias were given the standard temperate day scheme introduced in 1937. Two Virginias at least were still flying on parachute testing trials during the Battle of Britain; J7710, one of them, was almost literally blown to bits when a gale on December 6 1940 broke it loose from its picketing, and J7434, the other machine, survived until late 1941 when it undershot on landing at Henlow.

In the mid-1930s these two Virginias, with two others, were given an overall roundel red finishing scheme, to give warning of their parachute droppings. After war was declared and the green/brown finish for upper-surfaces appertained, the under-surfaces were in yellow. This was the finish for trainers, but was extended to various miscellaneous types for home defence identification purposes—the Virginias hardly qualifying as a well-known aircraft by 1940.

Unit markings

Although formation flying did not apply at night, by day it was a regular part of training in night bomber units. Since the individual serial numbers, marked as with other aircraft of the period on rear fuselage and rudder, were in black on dull green, some more distinctive individual identity marking was needed. In practically all squadrons this was given by an individual letter, painted both sides, fore and mid-fuselage.

The establishment of most heavy bomber squadrons between the wars was ten aircraft organised into two flights, so that from December 1924 when flight colours were authorised by the Air Ministry, only two colours were appropriate, red for 'A' and yellow for 'B' Flights.

At a time when aircraft were reckoned to average £2,000 apiece (£1,000 airframe + £1,000 engine), a Virginia at £14,000 was in a class of its own and considered worthy in some units of more than a mere number. Many were given names, some with all due ceremony. These were marked on nose and tail according to units as tabled on page 90. This is a trend now revived in the RAF for transport aircraft.

Another innovation on Virginias was a unit crest. Perhaps the very drab finish of these dull green monsters engendered a desire for embellishment —albeit discreetly within the bounds of night bomber camouflage. These crests are illustrated in Fig 18. It should be understood that they are the crests as marked on the aircraft, *not* the crests officially adopted in 1935 after the Office of Chester Herald was appointed Inspector of RAF Badges. Individual squadron markings were as follows:

No 7 Squadron: The early silver aircraft of 1924 had a small '7' marking as illustrated in Fig 18 about 12 inches diameter in black on each side of the nose. When in Nivo finish, a unit crest and motto were placed centrally on the nose.

A unit letter was displayed on the nose and on a fuselage panel as drawn in Fig 17. Other examples in 1927 were—'A' Flight: 'A' J8241, 'B' J8329, 'C' J8240, 'D' J6856, and 'B' Flight: 'J' J8328. Aircraft in the squadron were named, examples being *Taurus* and *Polaris*.

No 9 Squadron: Like No 7 Squadron, this squadron had individual identity letters on the nose and mid-fuselage in flight colours but without the panels. Examples are 'D' K2655, 'M' J7275, 'U' J7711 and 'Y' K7716.

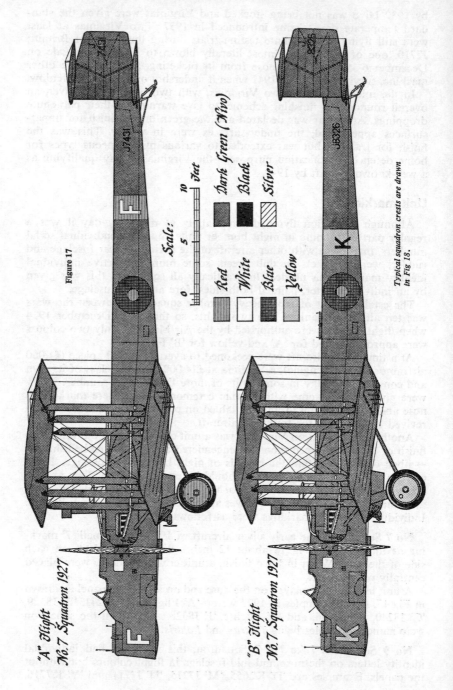

Figure 17

Scale:

0 5 10 Feet

Dark Green (Nivo)

Black

Silver

Red

White

Blue

Yellow

Typical squadron crests are drawn
in Fig 18.

"A" Flight
No. 7 Squadron 1927

"B" Flight
No. 7 Squadron 1927

88

No.7 Squadron (1924)   *No.7 Squadron (1931)*   *No.10 Squadron*

PER DIEM PER NOCTEM

I V O

No. 500 Squadron   *No. 502 Squadron*

500

QUO FATA VOCENT

Figure 18: *Unit crests displayed by Virginias in service.*

NIHIL TIMEO

At one period a six-inch band was painted around the rear fuselage in flight colours as representative of the squadron's markings in the First World War.

Naming of the aircraft was started in 1927 with Kings and Queens of Wessex as the theme; K2664 'K' was *Caedwalla of Wessex*. Proper nameplates were made and affixed centrally on the nose.

No 10 Squadron: Individual letters were marked on the side of the nose only with the squadron crest centrally on the nose (eg, 'N' K2674).

No 58 Squadron: Individual letters were painted on the nose and midfuselage in flight colours; 'B' Flight examples are 'U' J8914 and 'V' K2676.

No 500 (County of Kent) Squadron: Although numbered first in the Special Reserve squadrons, No 500 did not form first, and when its initial establishment of eight Virginias and two Avro 504Ns was approved in October 1932, the aircraft marking styles were not based on Virginias in regular RAF squadrons, but on aircraft in other Special Reserve units. Since No 501 marked its squadron number, black on the silver finishes of its Wallaces, No 500 marked its number clearly in white on the fuselage of their dull green Virginias. In effect this was a day bomber marking on a night bomber unit. The marking of individual letters was based on No 7 Squadron.

By the squadron's very name, their crest was logically the prancing horse of the County Arms of Kent. Their aircraft names, painted on each side of the nose and centrally on the rear turret, were those of Kentish locations, eg, 'A' J8240 *Isle of Thanet,* and 'B' J7566 *City of Canterbury.*

No 502 (Ulster) Squadron: Another Special Reserve unit with territorial associations, No 502 marked the Red Hand symbol of Ulster on a white shield background on each side of the nose of their Virginias.

Serial markings

The official airframe number was marked on both sides of the rear of the fuselage in black 8-inch digits and repeated similarly on both sides of both rudders. Up to March 17 1927, serials were not marked under the wings, but on that date orders were given that serials would be marked in white 4-inch strokes on the wing under-surfaces of night bombers, in characters $2\frac{1}{2}$ feet high and $1\frac{1}{2}$ feet wide, giving at least one foot clearance from the wing roundels. The numbers on starboard and port wings were to read from opposite ways.

Serial number	Sequence of mark numbers as built and subsequent conversions	Known squadron service
J6856	I-VII-VIII-VII-X (First flew, 24.11.22)	7, 9
J6857	II-VII-X	7, 58
J6992	III-VII-IX-X	7, 9
J6993	III-VI-IX (No 7 Hendon Air Pageant, 1923)	9
J7129	III-VII-X	7, 9
J7130	III-VII-IX-X	7
J7131	III-VII-IX-X	7, 58
J7132	III-VII-IX-X	7, 9, 58
J7274	IV-VII-IX	
J7275	IV-VII-X	9
J7418	V-VI	
J7419	V-VIII-X	7
J7420	V-VII-X	9
J7421	V-VII-X	9, 58
J7422	V-VI-VII-X	9, 58
J7423	V-VI-IX	
J7424	V-VII-X	
J7425	V-VII (Ditched, Thames Estuary, 21.3.27)	9
J7426	V-VII	9
J7427	V-VII-X	7, 9, 58
J7428	V-VII-IX-X	58
J7429	V-VII-X	9, 58
J7430	V-VII-X	10, 58
J7431	V-VII	7
J7432	V-VII	
J7433	V-VII-X (Crashed, 2.5.28)	9
J7434	V-VII-X (Undershot Henlow, 4.9.41)	7, 9, 58, 214
J7435	V-VII-IX	
J7436	V-VII-IX-X	58
J7437	V-VI-IX-X	9, 58
J7438	V-VI-VII-IX-X	58, 500
J7439	V-VI-VII-X	9
J7558	VI-IX	15
J7559	VI-VII-X	7, 9
J7560	VI-X	9, 502
J7561	VI-VII-IX-X (Crashed near Manston, 4.11.30)	9
J7562	VI-IX-X	9
J7563	VI-IX-X	
J7564	VI-IX	9
J7565	VI-VII-X	9

Serial number	Sequence of mark numbers as built and subsequent conversions	Known squadron service
J7566	VI-VII-X (Named *City of Canterbury*)	58, 500
J7567	VI-IX-X	7, 9
J7706	VI-VII-X	9, 502
J7707	VI-IX	
J7708	VI-IX-X	9
J7709	VI-IX (Crashed, 24.3.30)	58
J7710	VI-VII-X (Wrecked in gale, 6.12.40)	9, 58
J7711	VI-VII-IX-X	9
J7712	VI-VII	9
J7713	VI-VII	
J7714	VI (Crashed, 19.4.27, at Eastchurch)	9
J7715	VI-IX-X	7, 9
J7716	VI-IX	9, 58
J7717	VI-X	15
J7718	VI-IX-X	58
J7719	VI-IX-X	9
J7720	VI-IX	
J8236	VII-IX (Used as engine test-bed)	7
J8237	VII-X (Crashed, 7.10.32)	
J8238	VII-X	7, 9, 502
J8239	VII (Crashed, 14.3.28)	9
J8240	VII-IX-X (Named *Isle of Thanet*)	7, 500
J8241	VII-X (Crashed, 19.1.31, at Worthy Down)	7
J8326	VII-X	7
J8327	VII	9
J8328	VII-X	7, 58, 502
J8329	VII-X	7
J8330	VII-X	
J8907	IX-X	10, 58
J8908	IX-X	9, 214
J8909	IX	
J8910	IX-X	
J8911	IX	7
J8912	IX-X	9
J8913	IX-X	7
J8914	IX-X	58
K2321	X (Struck-off-charge, 22.5.35)	
K2322	X (Struck-off-charge, 31.11.34)	
K2323	X (Flown away for scrap, April 1935)	502
K2324	X (Sold as scrap, February 1938)	58, 502
K2325	X (Struck-off-charge, January 1937)	
K2326	X (Struck-off-charge, 27.8.35)	
K2327	X (Struck-off-charge, 18.11.38)	RAF Henlow
K2328	X (Struck-off-charge, July 1935)	
K2329	X (Crashed, 21.3.40)	RAF Henlow
K2330	X (Struck-off-charge, 8.4.37)	9, 500, 215
K2331	X	10 ('A' Flight)
K2332	X (Struck-off-charge, 24.7.33)	10 ('B' Flight)
K2333	X (Struck-off-charge, 4.1.37)	10, 58, 502
K2334	X (Sold as scrap, November 1937)	58, 51
K2335	X (Struck-off-charge, 2.5.35)	502
K2336	X (Flown away for scrap, April 1935)	58, 502
K2337	X (Struck-off-charge, January 1937)	58
K2338	X (Struck-off-charge, 29.6.34)	502
K2339	X	502
K2650	X	7, 502
K2651	X	9
K2652	X	
K2653	X	7, 502
K2654	X	9

Serial number	Sequence of mark numbers as built and subsequent conversions	Known squadron service
K2655	X (Letter 'D' in 9 Sqn)	9
K2656	X (Struck-off-charge, 2.4.37)	9, 214
K2657	X (Struck-off-charge, 18.8.37)	214
K2658	X (Stored and sold, April 1936)	7
K2659	X (Stored, struck-off-charge, 17.5.34)	
K2660	X (Struck-off-charge, 4.1.37)	9, 214
K2661	X (Stored until disposal, 22.4.36)	
K2662	X (Struck-off-charge, 29.5.36)	9, 10
K2663	X (Struck-off-charge, 23.5.34)	
K2664	X (Struck-off-charge, 4.1.37)	9, 214
K2665	X (Struck-off-charge, 4.1.37)	214
K2666	X (Sold as scrap, 21.2.38)	51, 58
K2667	X (Struck-off-charge, 23.7.34)	500
K2668	X (Letter 'K' in 500 Sqn)	500
K2669	X (Sold as scrap, 30.11.37)	215, 51, 500
K2670	X (Struck-off-charge, 17.9.35)	
K2671	X (Caught fire, July 1935)	9
K2672	X (Struck-off-charge, 30.11.37)	215, 75
K2673	X (Caught fire, October 1935)	9
K2674	X (Letter 'N' in 10 Sqn)	10, 58
K2675	X (Struck-off-charge, 10.9.35)	58
K2676	X (Struck-off-charge, 21.1.38)	58
K2677	X (Struck-off-charge, ex-store, 8.4.37)	
K2678	X (Struck-off-charge, 30.11.37)	215
K2679	X (Struck-off-charge, 1.6.35)	9, 58
K2680	X (Sold as scrap, 30.11.37)	214, 500

Chapter 13

Handley Page second generation night bombers—Hyderabad and Hinaidi

CONTEMPORARIES OF THE VIRGINIA, the Hyderabad and Hinaidi, also night bombers, bore similar colouring and markings; but whereas the Virginia retained its name through successive developments, the Napier Lion-powered Hyderabad, when re-engined with Bristol Jupiters, became the Hinaidi. Visually, this was a difference of in-line and radial engines.

The first Hinaidis, re-engined Hyderabads, were designated Mk I and the production all-metal framed Hinaidis became Mk II.

General finishes

Named after military stations in India and Iraq respectively, both Hyderabads and Hinaidis were restricted to home service, with the exception of a single Hinaidi. Their overall service was limited to the years 1924-37, a period when Nivo finishes were standard for night bombers.

The prototype Hyderabad appeared in October 1924 in silver (aluminium pigment) finish, but all production Hyderabads and Hinaidis were given an overall Nivo finish of a dull green sheen with night roundels of red inners and blue outers, excluding all white.

The prototype Hinaidi was finished in Nivo since it was service Hyderabad J7745 re-engined with Jupiters. But when this aircraft was out in India for tropical trials, it was given an overall silver (aluminium) finish.

Hyderabads were declared obsolete in August 1934 and Hinaidis in 1937.

Squadron markings

In spite of the rigid economies of the 1920s, successive governments were aware of the desirability of keeping alive a thriving British aircraft industry and Handley Page, the longest to survive of the independent British aircraft manufacturers and only recently going into liquidation, was steered through the 1920s by the placing of limited orders, sufficient to equip two first-line squadrons, Nos 10 and 99, with Hyderabads and replace them, in the same squadrons, in the early 1930s with Hinaidis.

Both squadrons were maintained at a two-flight basis of five aircraft per flight and thus only the 'A' and 'B' Flight colours of red and yellow respectively were used. Unlike the Virginia squadrons, individual letters on the nose were not repeated on fuselage sides. Individual squadron schemes were as on page 95.

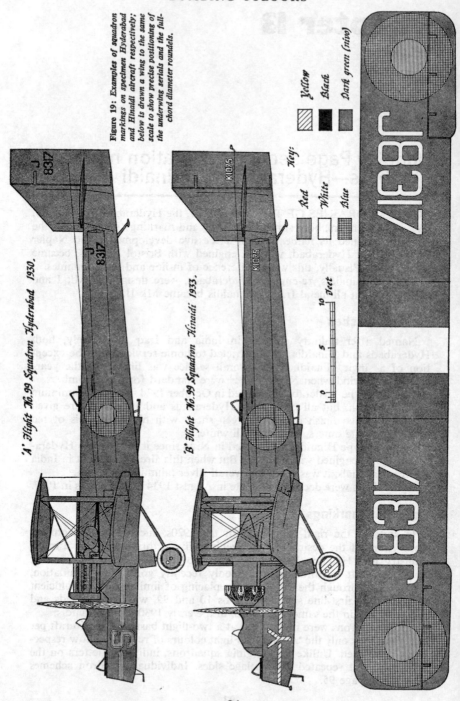

Figure 19: Examples of squadron markings on specimen Hyderabad and Hinaidi aircraft respectively; below is drawn a wing to the same scale to show precise positioning of the underwing serials and the full-chord diameter roundels.

Key:

Red
White
Blue

Yellow
Black
Dark green (olive)

'A' Flight No. 99 Squadron Hyderabad 1930.

'B' Flight No. 99 Squadron Hinaidi 1933.

No 10 Squadron: Crest of squadron, as illustrated in the previous chapter for this squadron's Virginias, was positioned on nose of Hyderabads and later Hinaidis. Large white individual letter was placed on each side of the nose, eg, Hyderabad J8805 was 'C' and J8810 'E'; Hinaidi K1919 was 'H' of 'B' Flight.

In the early 1930s the Squadron Commanding Officer, Wing Commander A. T. Whitelock, an ardent Latin scholar, introduced the squadron crest and motto which were marked on the nose of their aircraft. The crest was in the form shown for the unit's Virginias which replaced their Hinaidis. However, on the Hinaidis the motto also appeared. This was *Rem acu tangere*, meaning 'to touch the matter with the point of a needle'—their aim in bombing.

That Virginias replaced the Hinaidis may suggest that this Handley Page bomber survey should have preceded the Virginia, but it should be appreciated that owing to continual improvements of the Virginias, through ten marks, they preceded and to an extent succeeded the Hinaidi.

No 99 Squadron: This squadron instituted a trim line around the nose of their Handley Pages, phased in with the aircraft's individual letter as illustrated. Both letter and trim were in the flight colour. Examples: Hyderabad's J8317 'S', J8320 'T', J8323 'D' and Hinaidi K1075 'Y'. The trim line was not instituted until the squadron had operated Hyderabads for some months; initially they were without the trim line as shown in the photograph on page 117.

No 502 Squadron: Aircraft of this squadron bore the Red Hand of Ulster symbol on the nose of their Hyderabads as shown in the previous chapter for the Virginia. Examples include J7739, J7742, J8808 and J8809.

No 503 Squadron: Aircraft of this Special Reserve squadron bore individual letters on each side of the nose and a crest on the tip. The crest was part of the Arms of Lincoln, a red cross of St George on a white shield, with a small central fleur-de-lys, and above the shield a white RAF eagle. Examples: Hyderabads J7752, J8807 and J9294; Hinaidis K1063 and K1066.

Serial markings

On Hyderabads serial numbers on the fuselage and rudder were in black with the prefix letter placed centrally above digits; on Hinaidis serials in these positions were in white and in line.

In March 1927, new Air Ministry instructions led to the introduction of serials under the wings, to be white on Nivo finishes in 2½-foot characters. In practice, however, they were painted twice that size on bombers. Since No 99, the first squadron to be equipped with Hyderabads, received them in April 1926 and No 10 Squadron, the next, not until January 1928 on re-formation, only No 99 had unmarked wings and only for a short period.

Chapter 14

The Boulton & Paul day bombers—Sidestrand and Overstrand

THE BOULTON & PAUL day bombers had a lineage that spanned the two world wars, but missed operational service in both; and the two types that reached squadron service, the Sidestrand and Overstrand, formed the complete equipment of only one RAF squadron, No 101.

The experimentals

Early in 1918 the design staff of Boulton & Paul, under J. D. North, put forward a high performance bomber project which was considered for three of the newly drafted RAF specifications, as a long or short range bomber and as a fighter reconnaissance. Production of three prototypes was recommended on April 15 1918. Unfortunately the planned power plants, twin Dragonflies, were having protracted teething troubles and not until late October or early November did the first fly. It was finished in the usual PC10 which in 1919 was changed to AMA.

The three prototype Bourges F2903-2905 were produced in various forms and were followed by a developed all-steel version, the Bolton J6584, and then a new twin-engined medium bomber, the Bugle, of which seven (J6984, J6985, J7235, J7259, J7260, J7266, J7267) were built and finished in the standard aluminium finish of the mid-1920s. Not until Boulton & Paul's fourth bomber type, the Sidestrand, ordered in 1927, did a production order result and this firm have an aircraft for squadron service.

General finish

No 101 Squadron re-formed at Bircham Newton on March 21 1928 with Sidestrands and operated two flights, 'A' and 'B', of four aircraft in each. For several years it remained the sole medium bomber squadron in the RAF. As a day bomber squadron, the finish of their aircraft was 'silver', to use the colloquial term for the finish. In fact the metal parts of the structure were sprayed with Air Ministry grey cellulose paint, and the fabric coverings were initially doped red (red oxide was a fabric protective) and given a final coating of aluminium pigmented dope.

Both Cellon and Titanine doping schemes were approved using red

57 *Vickers Virginia J6993 bearing the Park No 7 at the 1923 Hendon Air Pageant* (Ministry of Defence H353).

58 *Vickers Virginia J7566 of No 500 Squadron in standard Nivo finish* (via J. C. Strickland).

59 *Vickers Virginia J8240 of No 500 Squadron* (via J. C. Strickland).

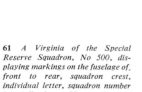

60 *Virginia J7715 in standard Nivo and night roundels photographed on May 19 1928, after being brought up to Mk IX standard* (Ministry of Defence 3398).

61 *A Virginia of the Special Reserve Squadron, No 500, displaying markings on the fuselage of, front to rear, squadron crest, individual letter, squadron number (partially obscured by wings), panel with individual letter repeated, and serial number (J7438)* (Ministry of Defence H1869).

97

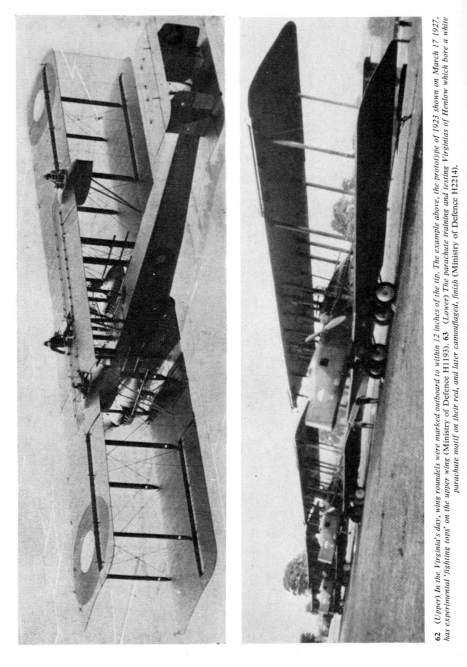

62 (*Upper*) *In the Virginia's day, wing roundels were marked outboard to within 12 inches of the tip. The example above, the prototype of 1923 shown on March 17 1927, has experimental 'fighting tops' on the upper wing (Ministry of Defence H1193).* **63** (*Lower*) *The parachute training and testing Virginias of Henlow which bore a white parachute motif on their red, and later camouflaged, finish (Ministry of Defence H2214).*

64 and 65 *Vickers Victoria IIIs of No 70 Squadron in Iraq, August 1926, before the overall silver became standard. The front fuselage of ply covering in battleship-grey contrasts with the silvery aluminium doped fabric to the rear. Vernons with the squadron at the time had overall silver finish and the wooden parts of the Victorias were soon painted aluminium to conform.*

66 *A named Vickers Vernon bearing the inscription* Pelican. *King Fiesal of Iraq is seated in the cockpit* (Ministry of Defence H884).

67 *A Vickers Valentia displays both underwing and fuselage side markings* (Ministry of Defence H499).

100

oxide pigment initially and aluminium finally. The actual scheme used was marked on all major components, wings, ailerons, fin, rudder, etc, as a suffix to the part number of the component, which appeared in $\frac{1}{4}$ inch stencilled characters. The suffix CX indicated Cellon Scheme 10 and T2S indicated Titanine Scheme 2 sprayed.

A large aircraft, indeed the largest of the day bombers in the RAF, the Sidestrand had a relatively large area of aluminium finish which, if it did not actually sparkle like silver in sunlight, did reflect light which could cause discomfort to the crew keeping a watchful lookout throughout a long flight. Since there was also a ventral gun position whose gunner could be similarly affected by light reflection from clouds on to the under-surface and by the sun's rays at dawn or nightfall, a dark matt green shaded area was made to extend along the top decking, over the nose and on the under-surface of the fuselage back to the tail. Engine nacelles were also painted matt dark green, not so much because they were a reflecting surface but because oil blown back from the engine did not show up as much on the darker surfaces.

With the Overstrand, the restful green was discarded in service versions as the pilot then had an enclosed cockpit of very slightly tinted anti-glare perspex and the turret gunner in the nose was completely free from reflecting surfaces.

Bearing day markings, these aircraft were subject to the important changes that occurred to the national markings of all RAF aircraft. It was notified on August 15 1930, that the order of colours on the rudder would be reversed. Since rudder striping had first been introduced in May 1915, it had always been blue from the rudder post, then white and red trailing. Now it was red from the rudder post, and this continues today with red leading on all fin flashes. The new instruction issued to contractors specified that the change would be effected on all aircraft delivered after September 29 1930. In service the red portion was to be overpainted blue and the blue overpainted red with a final coat of clear dope or varnish to fix and protect the paint. On all service aircraft, this had to be effected by the last day of October 1930.

Then followed another change. As the speed of aircraft increased, so the aerodynamic effects of the thickness of paint became more apparent and it was decided that control services should not be overpainted. This meant that roundel sizes were reduced so that they did not overlap on to ailerons, and rudder striping was discontinued altogether. This change was decreed from August 1 1934, and it became effective during the remaining months of the year.

Squadron markings

Sidestrands were ordered to equip one squadron, with the Overstrand later replacing them in that squadron. Consequently Sidestrand and Overstrand unit markings are mainly those of the squadron concerned, No 101. This unit was based at Bircham Newton, Norfolk, from March 1928 to October 1929, then at Andover, Hampshire, until November 1934, and then at Bicester, Oxfordshire, where it was re-equipped with Blenheims in the summer of 1938.

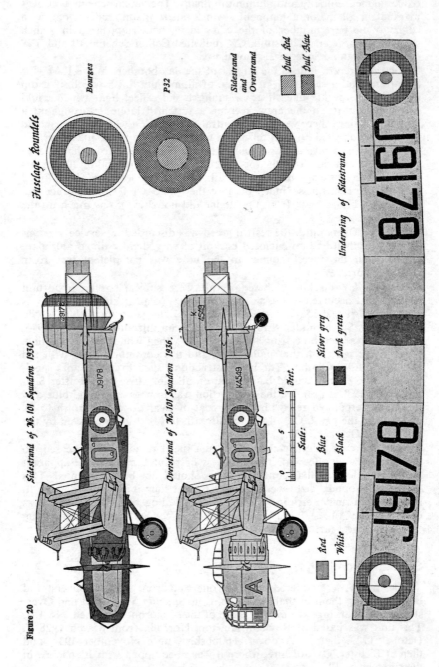

Fuselage Roundels

Bourges

P32

Sidestrand and Overstrand

Dull Red
Dull Blue

Underwing of Sidestrand

Figure 20

Sidestrand of No. 101 Squadron 1930.

Overstrand of No. 101 Squadron 1936.

Scale: 0 5 10 Feet.

Red
White
Blue
Black
Silver grey
Dark green

As a day bomber squadron, it marked its squadron number 101 on the fuselage side, and as the largest day bomber operator, the squadron marked its number correspondingly large. To give the aircraft some colour within the rigid regulations, the '101' was painted in the officially approved flight colours, red for 'A' Flight, yellow for 'B' Flight and blue for 'C' Flight. However, for the most part, the squadron operated on a two-flight basis of four aircraft in each flight. A 'C' Flight was only formed for a short period in 1935 when the first Overstrands were on service trials alongside 'A' and 'B' Flights of Sidestrands, and for a short period later under the 1935 Expansion Scheme. Thus the '101' marking was, in the main, either in red or yellow.

Aircraft in the squadron were marked with an individual letter on each side of the nose, also in the flight colour. On Sidestrands the letter was small and on Overstrands large.

Serial numbers

Marked in the conventional positions of the period, on the rear of the fuselage, on the rudder and under the wings as illustrated in Fig 20, the serial numbers appeared in black. The range of numbers used, the individual markings and history of the individual aircraft were as follows:

Serial	Type	Details of service and markings
J7938	Sidestrand I	Served at Martlesham Heath and to No 101 Sqn, April 20 1928
J7939	Sidestrand I	Used by No 15 Sqn at Martlesham Heath. To No 101 Sqn, April 18 1928
J9176	Sidestrand II	Marked 'F' of No 101 Sqn from March 15 1929 until crashed at Gosport, November 22 1929
J9177	Sidestrand III	Served in No 101 Sqn from delivery on March 7 1929
J9178	Sidestrand II	'A' of 101 Sqn crashed on take-off, April 25 1929, and was rebuilt as Mk III
J9179	Sidestrand II conv to Overstrand	2nd of type in No 101 Sqn as aircraft letter 'B'. Crashed at Bicester, March 30 1936
J9180	Sidestrand II/III	Collected May 29 1929. Crashed into tree at Catfoss, May 5 1930
J9181	Sidestrand II	Collected July 13 1929. Crashed on landing, August 20 1929
J9185	Overstrand prototype	'P' of No 101 Sqn. Crashed at North Coates Fitties, September 9 1935
J9186	Overstrand prototype	Development aircraft. Bore black Park No 13 at Hendon
J9187	Sidestrand II/III	Served in No 101 Sqn, marked with red 'E'
J9188	Sidestrand II/III	Delivered September 19 1929. Served as 'C' of No 101 Sqn
J9189	Sidestrand II/III	Was 'G' of No 101 Sqn
J9767	Sidestrand III	Presumed delivered to store
J9768	Sidestrand III	Served in No 101 Sqn. Crashed on endurance test, March 5 1933
J9769	Sidestrand III	Served in No 101 Sqn marked with yellow 'G' and '101'
J9770	Sidestrand III	Converted to Overstrand and used for development work. No known unit markings
K1992	Sidestrand II/III	Delivered to store
K1993	Sidestrand II/III	'E' of No 101 Sqn
K1994	Sidestrand II/III	First with auto pilot. Replaced J7939 with No 15 Sqn

Serial	Type	Details of service and markings
K4546	Overstrand	Marked 'W' in No 101 Sqn. Crash landed at Bicester, June 11 1937
K4547	Overstrand	No 101 Sqn service October 1935 to September 1936 when placed in store
K4348	Overstrand	Served in No 101 Sqn until 1938 when placed in store
K4549	Overstrand	Served in No 101 Sqn, marked with 'A' and '101' in red
K4550	Overstrand	Served in No 101 Sqn until 1938 when placed in store
K4551	Overstrand	Marked with red 'C' and '101' in No 101 Sqn. Later in No 2 Air Observers' School
K4552	Overstrand	Held in store. Withdrawn 1940 as instructional airframe marked 1822M
K4553	Overstrand	Marked with blue 'Y' and '101' in No 101 Sqn
K4554	Overstrand	Served in No 101 Sqn. Scrapped in 1939
K4555	Overstrand	Served in No 101 Sqn. Scrapped in 1939
K4556	Overstrand	Marked 'F' and '101' in No 101 Sqn
K4557	Overstrand	Served in No 101 Sqn, then in No 2 Air Observers' School
K4558	Overstrand	Served in No 101 Sqn. Became 2146M as ground instructional airframe
K4559	Overstrand	'Y' of No 101 Sqn, later used for experimental work
K4560	Overstrand	Served in No 101 Sqn. Scrapped in 1939
K4561	Overstrand	Marked with green 'U' and '101' in No 101 Sqn
K4562	Overstrand	In No 101 Sqn until November 2 1936 when wrecked landing at Bicester
K4563	Overstrand	'I' of No 101 Sqn, ending up as Instructional Airframe No 2174M
K4564	Overstrand	No 101 Sqn until January 11 1937 when crashed in fog at Swanbourne, Bucks
K8173	Overstrand	No 101 Sqn then No 2 Air Observers' School. Crashed July 1940
K8174	Overstrand	'G' of No 101 Sqn then No 2 Air Observers' School. Scrapped 1940
K8175	Overstrand	Used by Aeroplane & Armament Experimental Establishment
K8176	Overstrand	Taken from store for No 104 Sqn. Used by various units
K8177	Overstrand	Last built, delivered to store, withdrawn 1940 as Instructional Airframe 2147M

(Sidestrand Mk Is were prototypes; Mks II and III differed by Jupiter VI and VIIIF engines respectively.)

NB: The form Boulton & Paul has been used since not until 1934 did the firm become Boulton Paul Aircraft. The company made one bid for a night bomber, and the single prototype produced, designated P32, was finished in Nivo with the appropriate night roundels. The P32 can be seen on page 159.

Chapter 15

Fairey day bombers—Fox, IIIF and Gordon

WITH THE LINES of a fighter, an American engine and a speed of over 150 mph that outstripped the fighters of its time, the Fox was favoured with a production order at a time of financial stringency. It followed the Fairey Aviation's Fawn (Chapter 11) and was in turn followed by the Fairey IIIF and Gordon day bombers that saw service up to the outbreak of war in 1939.

As day flying aircraft, all three types were subject to the reversal of colours of the rudder stripes on RAF aircraft during October 1930 as detailed in the previous chapter on the Sidestrand and Overstrand twin-engined day bombers. The following deletion of rudder striping in August 1934 affected only the IIIF and Gordon since the Fox was declared obsolete for RAF purposes in March 1933.

The Fairey IIIF was not discarded until 1940 and it was as late in the war as mid-1944 before the final Gordon was withdrawn, but these were not bomber versions. As a bomber, the Gordon was replaced in late 1937.

Fox

Like the twin-engined day-bombers, the Foxes were one-squadron aircraft, No 12, on which they left their mark for a fox insignia was then adopted as a squadron badge—and remains so today, for this squadron's Buccaneer S2s now bear foxhead insignia. They were a proud squadron. As one enthusiastic ex-member wrote, 'Other squadrons, fighter and bomber alike, were apt to be regarded with disdain; our Foxes could out-shine them all in all senses of the word. Our engine cowls and all bright parts had to glisten, and woe betide a fitter whose copper water pipes beneath the cowlings did not shine to a flight sergeant's satisfaction. I suppose we were dubbed "Shiny Twelve" with some justification.'

The fuselage and wings were fabric covered, protected by aluminium pigmented dope giving the aircraft a silvery appearance. The top decking of the fuselage in contrast, and possibly due to the glare produced by its shiny appearance, was painted a matt dark green.

Several of the Foxes had short lives. On one of the first formation practices by No 12 Squadron, on July 29 1926, two of their Foxes, J7942 and J7944, collided. Fortunately both pilots, jumping from 1,000 feet, landed safely by parachute. J7949 was next to crash through a throttle control becoming disconnected as it was about to land; it had to go back to Fairey's for re-building. Then J7951 crashed in a forced landing at Aston Rowant, Oxfordshire, in September 1927. So far, no crash had been fatal, and the crew of J7954, too, had a lucky escape when it caught fire at 2,000 feet on August 16 1928, and was landed in standing crops only a second or two before the main fuel tank exploded. Unfortunately, the next accident was fatal; this was on October 11 1928, when the tail came off J7946 over Hendon after diving in a salute to His Highness The Sultan of Oman.

A Curtiss D12 Felix engine from America in a British aircraft was a challenge to Rolls-Royce who designed their 'F' series which developed into the Kestrel. Three aircraft re-engined with the new Rolls-Royce joined the squadron from January 1929 as Mk IAs. Fairey works numbers which appeared by the side of the serial numbers on the fuselage were as follows:

Service serials	Fairey Nos	Conversions
J7941-7958	F847-864	J7945, J7947-7949 to Mk IA
J8423-8427	F875-879	J8424 became G-ACXX
J9025-9028	F952-955	J9026-9027 Mk IA
J9515	?	
J9834	F1138	Mk IIM all-metal. Became G-ABFG

In squadron service the Foxes initially bore the number 12 in a circle on the fin, replaced later by the foxhead insignia shown in Fig 21. During its last two years of service the squadron number was marked boldly on the fuselage side in the appropriate flight colour, 'A' Flight red, 'B' Flight yellow and 'C' Flight blue.

A surprising innovation in July 1929, during exercises with the Siskins of No 17 Squadron, was the doping of the upper-surfaces with Nivo (dark green). At this time the squadron had nine operational aircraft, six Mk 1s (Curtiss-engined) and three Mk 1As (Rolls-Royce-engined). This was deemed so efficient a camouflage that it was discontinued for flight safety reasons, lest it led to collisions.

Two ex-RAF Foxes, J7950 and J8424, as G-ACXO and G-ACXX, were entered in the 1934 England-Australia Air Race, the former arriving to become later VH-UTR in New Guinea, and the latter crashing and burning out en route. A Fox III three-seat day bomber was built (F1842) which bore the civil registration G-ABYY before being sent as a demonstration aircraft to China.

Fairey IIIF

The Fairey IIIF was produced as a spotter/reconnaissance aircraft for the Fleet Air Arm and as a general purpose aircraft for the Royal Air Force. As such these aircraft in general are not appropriate to this book, except for those allocated to Nos 35 and 207 Squadrons where they functioned in a day bomber role from Bircham Newton, 1929-32.

Fairey IIIFs allotted to the bomber squadrons were of the Mk I or Mk IV (General Purpose) type. In No 35 Squadron they replaced the DH9As in the three flights, four in each. 'A' and 'B' Flights received theirs

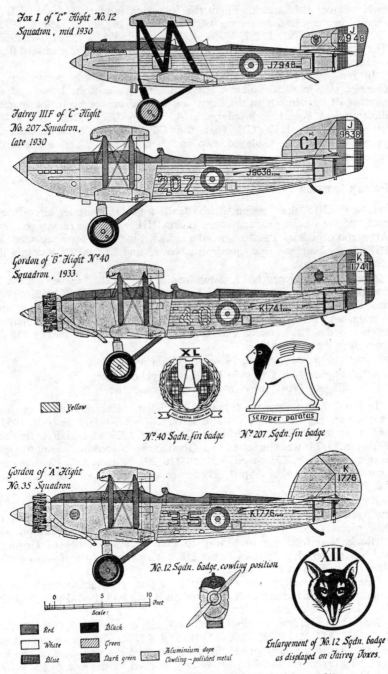

Fox 1 of "C" Flight No.12 Squadron, mid 1930

Fairey IIIF of "C" Flight No. 207 Squadron, late 1930

Gordon of "B" Flight Nº 40 Squadron, 1933.

Yellow

Nº 40 Sqdn. fin badge

Nº 207 Sqdn. fin badge

Gordon of "A" Flight No. 35 Squadron

No. 12 Sqdn. badge, cowling position

Scale:

Red · Black

White · Green

Blue · Dark green

Aluminium dope
Cowling – polished metal

Enlargement of No. 12 Sqdn. badge as displayed on Fairey Foxes.

Figure 21: *Typical Fox, Gordon, and Fairey IIIF aircraft in squadron markings.*

in November 1929 and 'C' Flight the following January. Individual IIIFs serving in the squadron during 1929-32 were J9167, J9171, J9784, J9785, J9787, J9788, J9791, J9797, J9798, J9799, J9800, J9820, J9821 and J9822. They bore the squadron number on the fuselage side in the standard flight colours as given for the Foxes of No 12 Squadron.

In No 207 Squadron, the unit number was similarly borne on the fuselage side in flight colours, but additionally the flight letter and the number of the aircraft in the flight was carried on the fin in the manner illustrated in Fig 21. Examples are 'A1' J9136, 'A2' S1202, 'A3' S1182, 'B1' S1205, 'B4' S1179, 'C1' J9638 and 'C2' S1203. On some aircraft the squadron crest was displayed, two inches high, above and between the letter and number on the fin.

Fairey Gordon

Like the IIIF, the Gordon was basically a general purpose aircraft and many of the service Gordons were Fairey IIIF airframes re-engined with Armstrong Siddeley Panther radial engines. Since Gordons replaced the IIIFs in the bombing role squadrons, Nos 35 and 207, they fall within the scope of this book.

Gordons re-equipped No 35 Squadron in July 1932. They were lucky in that their initial equipment was relatively new. Only K1163, K1762, K1776, and K1778 had been IIIFs and these had only been stored before conversion, and K2683-2690 were newly-built as Gordons. Each of their 12 aircraft had a small disc on each side of the nose, as illustrated in Fig 21, marked in the manner:

'A' Flight: Nos 1 to 4 in white within a red disc;
'B' Flight: Nos 1 to 4 in black on a yellow disc;
'C' Flight: Nos 1 to 4 in black on a blue disc.

In No 207 Squadron the former flight letter/number system prevailed; examples were: 'A4' K2691, 'B2' K1167, 'C1' K1757. One aircraft, J9651, had gone to No 207 Squadron in December 1929 as a IIIF to replace J9058; in 1932 it was converted to a Gordon and placed in store until withdrawn in August 1935 to go back to No 207 Squadron in its new configuration. It was sold in April 1939 for service in the then Royal Egyptian Air Force.

Both squadrons, Nos 35 and 207, were sent to the Sudan in late 1935 during the Abyssinian crisis and returned to the UK in 1936. Many of their aircraft were left in the Middle East and No 207 Squadron was particularly unfortunate in having to take over a number of Gordons which had been shipped back to the UK after several years of service with No 47 Squadron in the Sudan.

One other squadron had Gordons in a purely bombing role—No 40 Squadron which formed with the type on April 1 1931, and was thus the first Gordon squadron.

Individual Gordons serving in No 40 Squadron were K1736, K1740, K1741, K1743, K1748, K2700, K2701, and K2758. These bore the squadron number in the appropriate flight colours and the unit crest on the fin.

The Fairey works number was visibly marked by the side of the serial. A table of serial and corresponding works numbers is given as follows:

Service Nos	Fairey Nos	Original Type
S1168-1207	F892-931	IIIF Mk I
J9053-9077	F969-975, 980-997	IIIF Mk IVM
J9132-9174	F998-1040	IIIF Mk IV (GP)
J9637-9681	F1139-1183	IIIF Mk IV (GP)
J9784-9831	F1184-1231	IIIF Mk IV (GP)
K1158-1170	F1302-1314	IIIF Mk IV (GP)
K1697-1720	F1396-1419	IIIF Mk IVB (GP)
K1721-1728	F1420-1427	IIIF Mk IVB (GP) converted to Gordon on production line
K1729-1748	F1428-1447	Gordon I
K1749-1778	F1448-1477	III Mk IVB
K2683-2769	F1755-1841	Gordon I
K3986-4009	F1941-1964	Gordon II

NB: Many IIIFs subsequently converted to Gordons.

Chapter 16

Mainstay light bomber of the 1930s— Hawker Hart

THE HAWKER HART, which evolved from Specification 12/26 for a high performance day bomber, heralded a new era in British service aviation, for more aircraft of basic Hart design were built between the world wars in Britain than of any other design. Its variants included the Audax and Hector army co-operation aircraft, the Hardy general purpose machine and the Osprey for fleet spotting and reconnaissance.

Although basically a day bomber, it is a fact that the majority of Harts were not bombers at all. To meet the needs of RAF India a general purpose version was produced as the Hart (India); there was the unarmed Hart (Comm) for communications and later came the Hart (Inter), a standard Hart fitted out for training—an intermediate stage of the Hart (T) built as a high performance dual control trainer without military equipment and consequently the slight sweepback on the wings reduced to compensate for a revised centre of gravity.

Only the Hart (DB) comes within the scope of this book, for this is the version that armed the day bomber squadrons in Britain in the early and mid-1930s. They were built in considerable numbers and, by the sensible custom of the time, production was spread over several manufacturers to keep alive the British aircraft industry. So rigidly were service markings standardised at this time, that only their serial numbers indicated the factory of their origin. These are listed in the Appendices.

Additionally, certain aircraft ordered as Audax were completed to carry out the duties of Hart (DB) aircraft. These were known as Hart (Special). They differed *inter alia* by a fuselage three inches longer and braked undercarriage wheels. These aircraft, built by Gloster, were numbered K4365-4380, K4390, and K4407-4436.

All the numbers on all Harts were marked in black 8-inch characters, on both sides of the rear fuselage and both sides of the rudder, and underneath the wings inboard of the roundels, reading from the roundel in both cases, ie, one set was upside down relative to the other. The overall colours of the Hart (DB) day bombers were typical of their time. Engine cowlings were polished metal and fuselage and wing fabric coverings were doped aluminium. Coming into service in April 1930 and continuing in auxiliary squadrons until the late 1930s, the Hart went through all the national marking changes of the period; the order of the rudder stripes changed to red leading from the autumn of 1930 and then the striping was discarded altogether in the autumn of 1934. From this same time the wing roundels were reduced in size on re-doping so as not to overlap on to the ailerons.

In service, Harts were usually marked in a manner indicative of their squadron and flight. It had become traditional for bomber squadrons to mark their unit number on the fuselage side, normally in the colour of the particular flight to which they were allocated. Additionally, flight colours ('A' Flight red, 'B' Flight yellow and 'C' Flight blue) were painted on the wheel discs and may also have been painted, against regulations, on some spinners.

While representative aircraft for each unit are given by serial number it must not be assumed that a particular aircraft was always identified with a particular squadron, but only that at one period it served with the squadron stated. There was a flow of day bomber Harts from production to the day bombing squadrons in the UK from 1929-35. Following the Abyssinian crisis in 1935, when Britain was on the brink of war with Italy through the latter country's attack on Abyssinia, Harts were shipped out to the Middle East, some squadrons taking their own, some switching equipment and other Harts going direct from store to equip units on arrival. The crisis over, some Harts were returned to the UK where re-equipment of first-line Hart squadrons with Hinds had started, and Harts were then relegated to auxiliary squadrons. Finally, when the war came and the auxiliaries were re-armed, so the Harts were shipped to South Africa, after slight modification, to become trainers. There many were re-numbered in the South African Air Force and had the red in their roundels changed to orange.

Changes of units engendered changes in markings. It was not only the squadron numbers that were altered, for in the 1930s most RAF squadrons were adopting unit crests which were displayed, in general, on the fins of their aircraft. These were regularised from March 1935 when the Office of Chester Herald was appointed Inspector of RAF Badges. In February 1936, standard outline frames for marking these on aircraft fin surfaces were introduced, a grenade shape being allotted as appropriate for bomber squadrons; but by the time these had been introduced most Harts in squadron service had been replaced by Hinds, which are dealt with in the next chapter.

Markings of Hart (DB) day bombers in unit service are listed by squadrons, those from No 500 upwards being Auxiliary Air Force squadrons:

No 12 Squadron: Known as 'Shiny Twelve' by the immaculate appearance of their Foxes, No 12 Squadron maintained their high standards with their Harts which had highly buffed cowlings. Their unit number was displayed large in flight colours forward of the fuselage roundel and wheel discs were correspondingly coloured. Their foxhead insignia, as illustrated in Chapter 15, was marked centrally on fin surfaces in black. Harts that served in the squadron were: K1419, K1427, K1443, K1444, K1445, K1446, K2427, K2444, K2463, K3005, K3009, K3010, K3015 and K3019.

One of the 'showy' sidelines of this squadron was to have their wheel chocks (wooden blocks used to stay the aircraft while engines were run up) painted in flight colours with the number 12 in white on the facing surfaces.

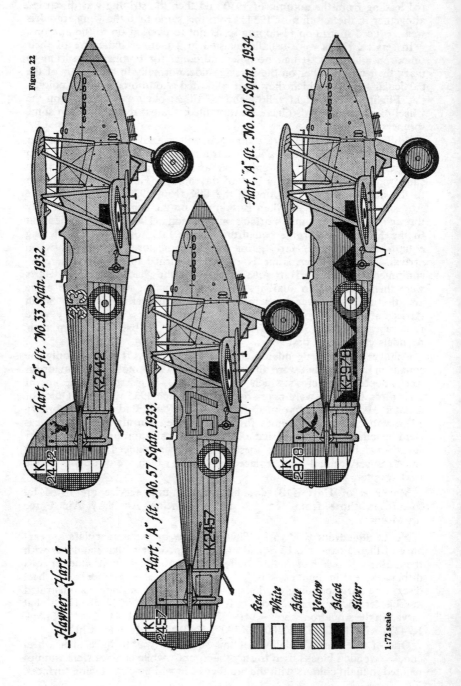

Figure 22

Hawker Hart I

Hart, "B" flt. No.33 Sqdn. 1932.

Hart, "A" flt. No.57 Sqdn. 1933.

Hart, "A" flt. No. 601 Sqdn. 1934.

Red
White
Blue
Yellow
Black
Silver

1:72 scale

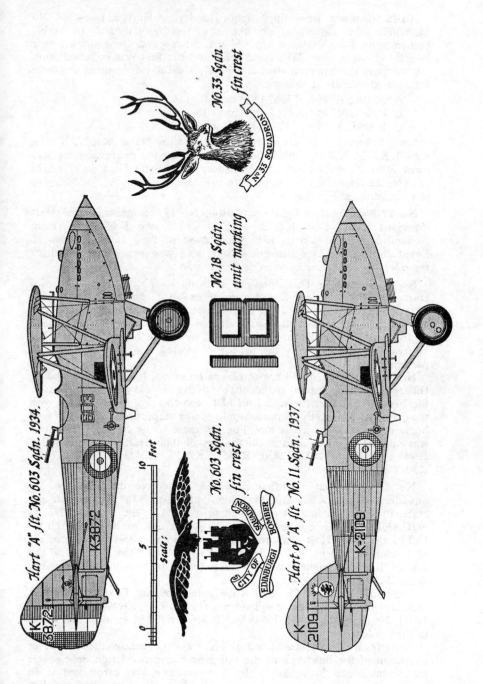

No.33 Sqdn.
fin crest

No.18 Sqdn.
unit marking

Hart "A" flt. No. 603 Sqdn. 1934.

K-3872

K 3872

Scale:

Feet

10

5

No.603 Sqdn.
fin crest

CITY OF EDINBURGH BOMBER

Hart of "A" flt. No. 11 Sqdn. 1937.

K-2118

K 2118

No 15 Squadron: Re-equipped from Horsleys to Harts in mid-1934. No 15, unlike other squadrons which marked their unit number in Arabic numerals, used the Roman form XV in flight colours. Their aircraft were initially all Armstrong Whitworth-built and the first was collected from the works at Coventry on June 2 1934. By the following spring the three flights used aircraft as follows:

'A' K3040, K3899, K3957 (XV in red);
'B' K3038, K3960, K3961 (XV in yellow);
'C' K3965, K3969, K3972 (XV in blue).

Until February 1936, when Hinds replaced the Harts, K3037, K3846, K3903, K3904, K3964, K3968 and K3971 were used as reserve and replacement aircraft and the Commanding Officer used K3900. Harts in 'C' Flight in 1936, the last to be re-equipped, were flown away from Abingdon to No 604 Squadron at Hendon.

No 17 Squadron: A fighter squadron, No 17, temporarily used Hart (Specials) K4366-4368, K4373, K4375, K4376 and K4421-4427 from November 1935 to March 1936 while most of their Bulldogs went to Egypt during the Abyssinian crisis. A Bulldog was retained in each flight for pilots to keep their hand in as fighter pilots.

No 18 Squadron: This squadron re-formed in November 1931 with Harts J9934, K1433 and K1434 arriving ex-No 33 Squadron on the 9th as their initial equipment. Their unit number in flight colours was marked smaller than standard on their aircraft, but what it lacked in size it made up for in finesse, for it was the only Hart squadron to present its number in stylised form; evidently the squadron boasted a signwriter among its personnel.

Noting that other squadrons displayed fin crests, No 18's Commanding Officer invited suggestions for a suitable design. It was pointed out that in the First World War the squadron had been the first to co-operate with the Cavalry Corps so that a horse would not be inappropriate and a winged horse even better, which is how Pegasus came to be chosen. This motif was marked in a shield form on the fins of their Harts, which included J9944, K2432, K2440, K2450, K2451, K2452, K2453, K2462, K2464, K3017 and K3046.

No 33 Squadron: The first squadron to receive the Hart, No 33 Squadron adopted a hart insignia which appeared on the fins of their aircraft. Presented at first as illustrated on page 113, the wording 'No 33 SQUADRON' was replaced after 1936 by the unit motto 'LOYALTY'. Unlike the other Hart squadrons, marking unit numbers forward or aft of fuselage roundels, No 33 chose to place it above the roundel. In the case of 'B' Flight, where the yellow did not show up well on the aluminium dope, the '33' was outlined in black.

Their first Harts, K9935 and K9937, delivered on February 25 1930, were the first Harts to enter squadron service; J9938, J9940, J9939, J9934, J9941, J9943, J9942, J9944, J9945 and J9946 arrived in the next two weeks in that order.

Harts from J9946 upwards had different flying characteristics due to an alteration of the incidence of the tailplane and a restriction on elevator movement. Since the squadron, by their training, was earmarked as an expeditionary force squadron in the event of an emergency, its J-serialled non-standard Harts were replaced by later standard aircraft. An emergency did come in 1935 with the Abyssinian crisis. The squadron was ordered abroad to the Middle East and under the overall reinforcement plan nine of the aircraft then held had to be handed over for shipment to Egypt for No 142 Squadron and the remaining seven of their aircraft had to be passed over to their station headquarters at Upper Heyford.

On arrival at Mersa Matruh in Egypt to patrol the border with Cyrenaica, then an Italian colony, the squadron was provided with 16 aircraft ex-No 142 Squadron: K4447-4456, K4484 and K4491-4495, plus K4475-4476 and K4478-4480 from store on war establishment reserve. In 1936, a flight was despatched to Palestine where Arab-Jew differences were again causing trouble. The squadron remained in the Middle East and in 1939 was made a fighter squadron and equipped with Gladiators.

No 40 Squadron: Re-equipping from Gordons to Harts in November 1935, No 40 Squadron is unique in that it was the only UK bomber squadron equipped with the Hart (Special) described above. Harts used were K4371-4372 and K4408-4420 delivered from production. These Harts bore their unit number in flight colours just forward of the fuselage roundels. In January 1936, the Harts of 'C' Flight had the figures '40' on the fuselages reversed and a '1' placed in front, when they became the nucleus of the reformed No 104 Squadron on their station—Abingdon. 'A' and 'B' Flights and a new 'C' Flight were supplied with Hinds in the following March.

No 57 Squadron: Reformed at Netheravon on October 20 1931 after service in the First World War. No 57's first aircraft were four Harts ex-No 12 Squadron. Harts known to have served in the squadron were J9940, J9941, K1422, K2429, K2446-2448, K2457-2458, K2465-2466, K3025 and K3032. These bore the number 57 boldly marked forward of the roundel, with the CO's aircraft having the number outlined in white.

In November 1935, the Rolls-Royce Kestrel IB engines in their Harts were replaced by Kestrel X engines, and in March 1936 the 'C' Flight Harts were taken off squadron strength and replaced by Hinds to form the nucleus of No 218 Squadron. This left the squadron with 'A' and 'B' Flights of six aircraft each until May when they were re-armed with Hinds.

No 142 Squadron: Reformed June 1 1934, the squadron was caught up in the Abyssinian emergency and sent to Egypt with three reserve aircraft plus nine aircraft from No 33 Squadron; while some of its own aircraft went to No 33 Squadron. In November 1936, the squadron returned home and reformed with Hinds.

During their service with the squadron, Harts bore the unit number 142 immediately forward of fuselage roundels. Harts serving the squadron included K3041-3043; K3840, K3842, K3843 and K3894 ex-33 Squadron; K3901 the first Hart to reach the squadron, and K3902, K3955, K3956, K3958, K3959, K3962, K3963, K3966, K3967 and K3970. (See 33 Sqn.)

No 500 (County of Kent) Squadron: From December 1935, this auxiliary squadron changed its role from a twin-engined night bomber squadron with Virginias, to a single-engined day bomber squadron with Harts. Auxiliary squadrons had a different establishment to regular squadrons and initially for No 500 it was six Harts (DB), one Hart (T) and two Avro 504Ns. In February 1937, the establishment was increased to nine Harts which was met by Harts K1423, K1428, K3018, K3050, K3053, K3816, K3845, K3848 and K4459.

No 501 (County of Gloucester) Squadron: This squadron used Harts from mid-1936 to early 1938. Their Harts were unusual in that their fuselage deckings were painted dark matt green following the pattern set by their earlier Wallaces. Harts concerned included K2438 and K2998.

No 503 (County of Lincoln) Squadron: This squadron changed its Wallaces for Harts in mid-1936, using K1423, K2428, K2447, K2450, K2457, K3007, K3017, K3023, K3030, K3034 and K3046.

No 600 (City of London) Squadron: Taking over Harts early in 1933 in place of Wapitis, this squadron apparently distinguished their aircraft by an absence of all but the mandatory service markings on K2473, K2979, K2980, K2981, K2982, K2985, K2986, K2987, K2988, K3028 and K3847.

No 601 (County of London) Squadron: When this squadron changed its Wallaces for Harts in early 1933, it continued to mark the unit winged sword insignia on fins, but stopped marking the unit number on fuselages.

In July 1934, the role of the squadron was changed to fighting, but pending re-equipment with Demons, their Harts were bedecked in fighting colours. Harts used were: K2966, K2970-2973, K2976-2979 and K2989.

No 602 (City of Glasgow) Squadron: When No 602 discarded Wapitis for Harts in 1934 they reduced the presentation of the unit number to serial number size, placed beneath the gunner's cockpit. A representation of the unit's tree crest was placed on the fins of their Harts, including K3054, K3866, K3875, K3897 and K3965.

No 603 (City of Edinburgh) Squadron: Changing from Wapitis in 1934, this squadron also reduced the presentation size of the unit number; but in 1-foot digits, beneath the gunner's cockpit, it was larger than the '602' on the other Scottish auxiliary squadron. The unit crest, the castle of the City Arms of Edinburgh under a winged eagle, appeared very small on the fins of Harts which the squadron used: K3052, K3859, K3864, K3872, K3880 and K3898.

No 604 (County of Middlesex) Squadron: As an interim from discarding Wapitis for Demons, in a change of role from bombing to fighting, the squadron used Harts K3893, K3895, K3896, K3969, K3972 and K4490.

No 605 (County of Warwick) Squadron: This squadron's former equipment of Wapitis probably conditioned the unit's fad for having green fuselage deckings when it took over Harts in late 1934. The unit badge, of a bear supporting a ragged staff, was marked very conspicuously on the fin as illustrated on page 140. Harts serving in the squadron were K2435, K2439, K2442, K2459, K2465, K2976, K3010, K3018 and K3890-3892.

No 609 (West Riding) Squadron: Formed February 1936, the squadron is known to have used Harts K1426 and K3839 before receiving Hinds.

No 610 (County of Chester) Squadron: Formed in February 1936; used Harts K2424, K2982, K3040, K3054, K3831, K3881 and K4441.

No 611 (West Lancashire) Squadron: Formed in February 1936, Harts K3817, K3819, K3851 and K3852 were collected by the squadron from Sealand in January 1936 and, in addition, K3029, K3044 and K3881 are known to have served with the squadron shortly afterwards.

68 *Vickers Valentia K3165 showing individual letter 'B' repeated on top wing centre-section.*

69 *Handley Page Hyderabad of No 99 Squadron showing the unadorned individual letter as originally marked.*

70 *Aircraft of No 99 Squadron, a few months later than the photo above, after the smart trim line had been adopted flanking the individual letters.*

71 *Roundels of red and blue were painted at the wing extremities, as displayed by this upturned Hinaidi of No 10 Squadron, J9300. The pilot, the sole occupant, escaped injury but not admonishment.*

117

72 and 73 *Prototype Hyderabad J6994 photographed in aluminium finish on May 12 1924 and, below, production Hyderabad J8810 at Hendon in 1930 in Nivo finish* (Ministry of Defence RTP 733 and H196).

74 and 75   Prototype Sidestrand J7938 before 'the dark green shading was extended to the fuselage under-surface and, below, prototype Overstrand J9186 showing proposed shading for the type which was not adopted (Ministry of Defence).

119

76 (Top left) The first production Sidestrand, J9176, with the dark green shading extended to the fuselage under-surface. **77** (Above) Squadron service Sidestrand J9187. Compared with the photo of J9176 (top left), it will be seen that this Sidestrand photograph was taken after the rudder striping reversal. **78** (Left) Boulton & Paul Overstrands of No 101 Squadron. Leading aircraft has squadron number in red colour of 'A' Flights.

Chapter 17

Interim bomber—Hawker Hind

THE HAWKER HIND was a refined Hawker Hart and its visual differences were slight. It had the more powerful Rolls-Royce Kestrel V which slightly altered the cowling shape; the rear cockpit for the gunner/bomber was improved with the gun ring cut down into the fuselage decking to afford the gunner greater protection from the slipstream, and a tail-wheel replaced a tailskid.

A total of 527 were supplied to the RAF as an interim between the Hart and the new monoplane bombers. The Harts were then relegated to training in the newly formed Volunteer Reserve training units. As such the Hind was the last of the bombers delivered in aluminium doping. Entering service in 1936, it escaped the national marking changes of the Harts and, in fact, it could be said in general that, when units changed their Harts for Hinds, only the serial numbers appeared to have changed. Unlike Hart production, Hinds were all built by the parent firm, Hawker Aircraft Ltd.

To summarise the markings on delivery, roundels on fuselage sides were standardised in size as illustrated in Fig 23; on wings, port and starboard sides, upper-surfaces of top wing and bottom-surface of lower wing, they were the maximum size permissible without overlapping the ailerons. Serial numbers were in black 8-inch characters on rear fuselage and rudders, and were also painted underneath the wings inboard of the roundels.

On reaching squadrons in the newly formed and rapidly expanding Bomber Command, they would be conspicuously marked with the unit number in their flight colours, red for 'A' Flights, yellow for 'B' Flights and blue for 'C' Flights. Of these, yellow contrasted poorly against the silver finish and in this case the number was usually outlined thinly in black.

In squadrons in the mid-1930s there had been a trend towards adopting crests and some units marked these on the fins of their Harts. The practice continued in some Hind squadrons in a rather different way—the crests being contained in a standard frame. This was another move towards standardising markings. As the war clouds gathered over Europe, preparations were made to restrict markings so that if war came they could easily be obliterated as a security measure for units forming the Expeditionary Force. On February 1 1936 it was decreed that in future unit markings should be limited to the form of the unit's crest in a standard frame, a six-point star for army co-operation squadrons, a spearhead for fighter squadrons and a grenade form for bomber squadrons. The inside of the frame was to be painted white and the amount of colour and embellishment to the unit crest was up to the unit.

By the very wording of the instruction on unit markings, that they would be 'limited to' this form, as apart from 'will be displayed' in this form, they were taken to be optional markings. As the Hind was interim equipment of many reformed squadrons, pending delivery of Blenheims or Hampdens, not all units adopted fin markings.

The new monoplane bombers were factory finished in a camouflage of a disruptive pattern of dark earth and dark green from April 1937. This finish did not apply to Hinds which were all delivered by the end of 1937. However, Hinds still in service at the time of the Munich crisis of September 1938 were given an overall painting in standard camouflage distempers of dark brown, green and grey. These finishes, applied by units, were intended only as a ground camouflage for airfield security.

Another innovation at the time of the crisis was the issue of code letters instead of unit numbers, but the code lettering system did not become mandatory until March 1939. By that time most squadrons had re-equipped with monoplane bombers and the Hinds had been passed on to auxiliary squadrons and, when discarded in turn, they were utilised in other ways.

General Aircraft of Heston were given a contract in 1938 to convert 124 Hinds to trainers; with a yellow finish they were issued to Elementary & Reserve Flying Training Schools. Similarly the late-production Hinds from L7202 left the works as trainers.

From 1940 to 1942 there was a general exodus of Hinds from the UK to Commonwealth countries, mainly South Africa, New Zealand and India. Several went to foreign air forces including 12 to Afghanistan; these were K5409, K5457, K5554, K6668, K6675, K6804, K6832, K6842, K6853, K6855, L7180 and L7181; two of these have now returned for display in British museums.

Squadrons of RAF Bomber Command using Hinds, with their period of use indicated in brackets, are given below. Unless otherwise stated it may be taken that the squadron number was displayed boldly in flight colours immediately forward of the fuselage roundel and in figures of a height approximately equal to that of the roundel diameter.

No 12 Squadron (October 1936-February 1938): This unit was re-equipped with Hinds on returning from the Middle East after the Abyssinian crisis, using K5394 (crashed at Calshot April 1 1937), K5395 (crashed July 16 1937), K5396, K5399, K5501, K5526, K5547, K5548, K5549 (crashed March 3 1937), K5550-5554, K5555 (crashed September 16 1937) and K5560.

No 15 Squadron (February 1936-June 1938): Converting from Harts to Hinds this squadron was again the only one that marked the unit number in Roman numbers, ie, as XV. Appropriately a hind was chosen as their crest and this was authorised in May 1936 as 'A Hind's head affrontee' The crest in the standard grenade shape was marked on the fins which were plain aluminium doped, except for flight leaders' aircraft which had their fins painted in flight colours. Hinds used were: K5413, K5414, K5421, K5430, K5431, K5439, K5540, K5449, K5450, K5456, K5460-5462, K5463 (destroyed in a flying accident on October 16 1936) and K5464.

No 18 Squadron (February 1936-May 1939): This squadron distinguished their Hinds, like the Harts they had used, by a 'signwriting' presentation of their unit number. Pegasus, their unit crest, displayed in a shield form of the squadron's choosing on their Harts, was placed within the standard grenade form on their Hinds.

During the Munich crisis the code letters GU were allotted. This squadron used Hinds for a much longer period than other squadrons. Those used, with 'fall-outs' before replacement noted, were: K5451, K5452 (crashed August 10 1937), K5453 (crashed April 21 1937), K5454 (crashed February 11 1938), K5471, K5472 (crashed March 22 1937), K5473, K5474 (crashed January 2 1937), K5475, K5476, K5481, K5483-5486, K5487 (crashed April 24 1937), K5488, L7186 and L7193.

No 21 Squadron (December 1935-August 1938): The first Hinds to enter squadron service, K4637-4640, were sent to No 21 at Bircham Newton on the reformation of the squadron. Subsequent Hinds to bear the number 21 on their fuselage sides were: K4649, K5373, K5377, K5388 (crashed February 24 1937), K5446, K5518 (crashed August 26 1937), K6684 (crashed May 29 1937), K6685-6688, K6758-6759, L7175 and L7190-7191.

No 34 Squadron (January 1936-July 1938): Second of the bomber squadrons to get Hinds, No 34 first received K4642-4645 and K4650 on reforming with No 21 at Bircham Newton. The Hinds known to have borne the number '34' were K5393, K5397 (which ended its days at Tottenham County School), K5398, K5512-5513, K6689 (crashed December 12 1937), K6690, K6756 (which, after service as a glider tug and Air Transport Auxiliary 'hack' machine, survived until 1944) and K6757.

No 40 Squadron (March 1936-July 1938): From a markings view-point, when No 40 Squadron changed from Harts to Hinds it was only a case of a change of serial numbers, for the aircraft were marked precisely as previously described for their Harts. The Hinds used were: K5422-5427, K5428 (crashed October 8 1936), K5429 (withdrawn for No 15 Squadron), K5430-5433, K5437-5438, K5447-5448, K5470 (withdrawn for No 52 Squadron), K5495 and L7176.

No 44 Squadron (March-December 1937): Hinds used briefly while awaiting Blenheims were K5404-5405, K5407, K5415, K5418, K5420 and K5434-5435.

No 49 Squadron (February 1936-December 1938): Another of the squadrons reforming under the RAF Expansion Scheme with Hinds, No 49 marked their unit number slightly smaller and more forward on the fuselage than standard. The Hinds also bore the unit's greyhound crest in the standard grenade form on their fins. The first Hinds allotted were K4652, K5382-5385 but K5383 crashed early in 1937 after 135 hours flying. Others that followed were K5442-5443 and K6641 (ended up as Instructional airframe 1865M); K6642-6647 of which K6643, K6646 and K6647 were withdrawn before the replacement Hampdens arrived in late 1938, due to flying accidents; and K6752-6753, K6839 and L7194 (a replacement aircraft which itself crashed January 24 1938). During the 1938 summer crisis the code letters XU were allotted.

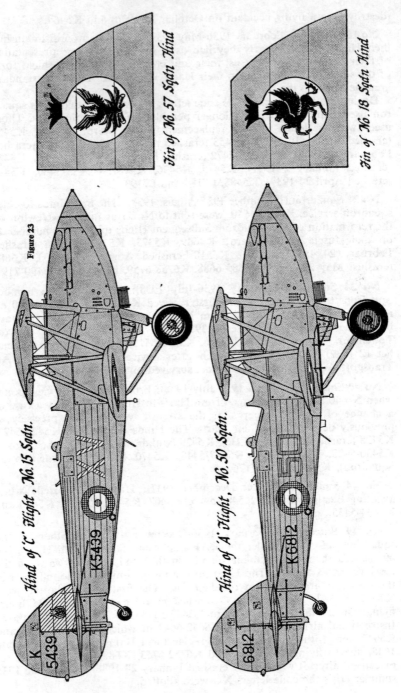

Fin of No. 57 Sqdn Hind

Fin of No. 18 Sqdn Hind

Figure 23

Hind of 'C' Flight, No. 15 Sqdn.

K5439

K 5439

Hind of 'A' Flight, No. 50 Sqdn.

K6812

K 6812

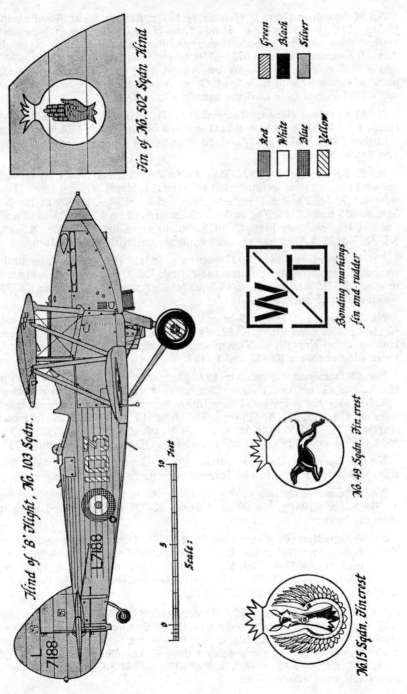

Fin of No. 502 Sqdn. Hind

Green
Black
Silver

Red
White
Blue
Yellow

W/T

Bonding markings
fin and rudder

Hind of 'B' Flight, No. 103 Sqdn.

No. 49 Sqdn. Fin crest

No. 15 Sqdn. Fincrest

Scale:

0   5   10 feet

L7188

7188

No 50 Squadron (June 1937-January 1939): Reforming at Waddington in May 1937, No 50 received Hinds from No 90 Squadron in June and marked these with a '50' only slightly smaller than the fuselage roundel. Aircraft concerned were: K6738-6750, all ex-90 Squadron of which K6746 and K6748 collided in mid-air on August 16 1937, but fortunately all occupants escaped with their lives. Other aircraft used were K6812-K6820 and L7195. Hinds later used the squadron code QX.

No 52 Squadron (January-December 1937): This squadron initially used Hinds K5406-5412 of which K5411 crashed in May 1937. Hinds to equip a further flight, K6734-6737, arrived later but by the end of the year the first Battles had arrived.

No 57 Squadron (May 1936-May 1938): As with Harts, so with Hinds, but with the unit crest as illustrated on page 124. Hinds arriving from May were K5477-5482 and K5489-5494, followed by K5406, K5409 ex-No 52 Sqn, K5455 and L7186. The first Blenheim arrived on March 25 1938 and the last Hind left on May 19 1938, but prior to the first date, K5479, K5482, K5489, K5494 had crashed while serving with the squadron.

No 62 Squadron (May 1937-February 1938): From reforming until receiving Blenheims the squadron used Hinds K6772-6784 from production to which K5415 was added, ex-44 Squadron, presumably to replace K6773 which crashed November 27 1937.

No 82 Squadron (June 1937-March 1938): On reforming No 82 received 12 Hinds from production, K6822-6833, of which K6822 and K6825 were both struck off strength on November 5 1937 suggesting that they collided. Later additions were K6842 and L7197.

No 83 Squadron (September 1936-December 1938): Reforming with Hinds, No 83 marked their unit number further forward than other squadrons so that it appeared beneath the gunner's cockpit. Aircraft used were K5416, K5525, K5528 (crashed June 13 1937), K5529 (crashed August 3 1937), K5530, K5556, K6634 (crashed April 7 1937), K6635-6640, K6754 and L7198. The unit code letters QQ were marked on in 1939.

No 88 Squadron (June-December 1937): Hinds K5451, K5496-5499, K6843-6848 and K6850 briefly formed this squadron's interim equipment.

No 90 Squadron (March 1937-May 1937): As an interim from reforming to Blenheims arriving, No 90 used Hinds K6738-6750 delivered straight from production.

No 98 Squadron (February 1936-June 1938): This squadron marked its Hinds boldly with '98' rather larger than roundel size on fuselage sides. Hinds used were K5368-5369, K5378 (crashed into the sea May 15 1936), K5379-5381, K5442; K5444, K5445 and K6613 which all crashed in 1937; K6614-6619, K6716-6719 and L7199-7200.

No 103 Squadron (August 1936-December 1938): This squadron marked '103' slightly smaller than roundel size. 'B' Flight aircraft had their yellow marking outlined thinly in black. K5519 was the first Hind to arrive at Andover and there was some delay before K5520-5524 arrived, followed by K5527, K5557, K6677-6683, K6719-6720, K6849 and L7188. The code letters GV were allotted later.

No 104 Squadron (January 1936-May 1938): Marking '104' boldly on their aircraft, this squadron received Hinds from the first batch, these being K4641, K4646-4648 and K4651 followed by K5514-5515, K6620-6626, K6721-6723 and L7201.

No 106 Squadron (Mid-1938): Temporarily used K5440, K5449 and K5450, all ex-15 Sqn.

No 107 Squadron (September 1936-September 1938): For two years No 107 used Hinds, marked with their unit number slightly smaller than roundel size. The Hinds were K4653-4654, K4655 (which crashed October 30 1936), K5419, K5543-5544, K5545 (crashed January 19 1937), K5558 (crashed December 13 1937), K6692-6698 (K6697 crashed August 19 1938), K6725 and K6731. The code letters BZ were allotted at the time of the Munich crisis at the same time as their first Blenheims arrived.

No 108 Squadron (January 1937-June 1938): This squadron marked its number in very bold strokes, but slightly smaller than roundel size, on its Hinds K6670-6676, K6724 and K6726-6730, supplemented later by K4648, K6775 and L7184-7185.

No 110 Squadron (May 1937-January 1938): Hinds were needed as an interim from reformation when K6809-6821 were used.

No 113 Squadron (May 1937-January 1939): Hinds K6796-6808 were allotted to this squadron on reforming and most of these were taken to the Middle East. Other aircraft used in the UK were K5420, K6824 and K6826. It is understood that the '113' markings were removed on all aircraft when shipped to the Middle East.

No 114 Squadron (December 1936-March 1937): In the brief period between reforming at Wyton and receiving Blenheims three months later, Hinds K5400-5403 were used.

No 139 Squadron (September 1936-July 1937): After forming at Wyton, Hinds K5370-5372, K5374-5376, K6710-6715, and K6733 were used with the number 139 displayed slightly smaller than roundel size, placed centrally outside the gunner's cockpit.

No 142 Squadron (January 1937-March 1938): Hinds K6654-6655 and K6657-6669 were initially allotted, but K6661, K6662, K6665 and K6667 did not survive to March 1938 when Battles started arriving.

No 185 Squadron (January-June 1938): Hinds used included K5424, K5426, K5427, K5495 and L7176, all from other squadrons.

No 211 Squadron (October 1937-May 1939): This squadron changed over from Audax to Hinds receiving K6851-6855 and L7174-7181, and later K6632-6633. The squadron number on the fuselage side was removed when the squadron embarked for the Middle East in 1938.

No 218 Squadron (March 1936-February 1938): The squadron marked their number in bold strokes slightly smaller than roundel size on Hinds K5372, K5389-5392, K5441, K5515-5516 and K6627-6633.

No 500 (County of Kent) Squadron (February 1937-March 1939): In 1937 the establishment of this auxiliary squadron was nine Hinds plus two Tutors. With the issue of Hinds K6699-6709 the unit was over-equipped but the establishment was raised in April 1938 to 12 Hinds following which

K5393 was added until March 1939 when Ansons were received and the unit's role changed.

No 501 (County of Gloucester) Squadron (January-November 1938): Hinds K5396, K5398-5399, K5410, K5550, K6690, K6782 (crashed June 12 1938), K6747, K6823, K6827-6829, K6831 and L7812 were used.

No 502 (Ulster) Squadron (April 1937-November 1938): Bearing the red hand of Ulster (see page 125) and '502' in flight colours, the Hinds of this squadron were initially K6761, K6763 (crashed November 14 1937) and K6764-6771, supplemented later by K5417, K6681, K6838 and L7197.

No 503 (County of Lincoln) Squadron (1938 only): Initially K6785-6795 were allotted, supplemented later by K5481 and L7193.

No 504 (County of Nottingham) Squadron (May 1937-October 1938): Hinds K6785-6795 went to the squadron straight from production, supplemented later by K5492, K6716, K6720, L7179 and L7199.

No 602 (City of Glasgow) Squadron (June 1936-November 1938): Numbers were marked as on Harts of this, the first auxiliary squadron to receive Hinds—these being K5500, K5502-5511 initially, supplemented later by K5418, K5460 and K5513.

No 603 (City of Edinburgh) Squadron (1938 only): Hinds K5498-5499, K6629, K6755, K6811, K6814-6817, K6819, K6843, K6845 and K6847 were used.

No 605 (County of Warwick) Squadron (August 1936-January 1939): The second auxiliary squadron to receive Hinds, this squadron received K5531-5541, supplemented later by K6674, K6676, K6710 and K6726.

No 609 (West Riding) Squadron (1938 only): The unit number was marked small by the pilot's cockpit on K5421, K5451, K5464, K5497, K5519, K5542, K6728, K6730, K6737, K6790, K6820, K6846, K6850, L7177, L7185 and L7188.

No 610 (County of Chester) Squadron (May 1938-February 1939): Used Hinds K5400, K5476, K6615, K6625-6626, K6659-6660, K6663-6664, K6718, K6721, L7186-7187 and L7190.

No 611 (West Lancashire) Squadron (1938 only): Used Hinds K5390, K5401, K5406, K5414, K5478 and K5480.

Chapter 18

Last of the biplane bombers—
Handley Page Heyford

LAST OF THE BIPLANE heavy bombers, the Heyfords had a fitting night bombing colour—the dull green known as Nivo. Similarly, so as not to compromise this camouflage colour, the roundels were of the night type without the white inner. The finish was unvarying throughout its flying life which started and all but ended in the 1930s.

The Heyford entered service with No 99 Squadron in November 1933 and Mks I, IA and II were declared obsolete in August 1939—the month before war was declared—and the Mk III in July 1941.

Unit markings

Night bombers, unlike the day bombers, did not display their squadron numbers on fuselage sides, but individual letters were marked on noses and fuselage sides in standard flight colours—'A' red, 'B' yellow and 'C' blue.

The use of individual letters was a functional necessity for formating in day exercises as the individual serial numbers did not stand out sufficiently well for this, but an additional marking exclusive in Bomber Command to Heyfords was a 'spat trim'. The idea is thought to have originated outside the command with the Vildebeest torpedo bomber/coastal patrol aircraft of No 22 Squadron. This squadron gave the wheel spats on its Vildebeests a colour flash and the Heyford squadrons, having aircraft with wheel spats, followed suit, using the same colours as for their individual letters.

One other unit marking used in some squadrons was the painting of the squadron crest on the nose. This was at the discretion of squadron commanders and was largely dependent on the artistic skill of a squadron member.

Serial numbers

Serial numbers, in the standard 8-inch black characters for all RAF aircraft, not only appeared 'lost' on the sheer bulk of the fuselage, but did not contrast well on the dark green. Under the wings the serials were marked large in white, but due to shadow this rarely shows up in photos

129

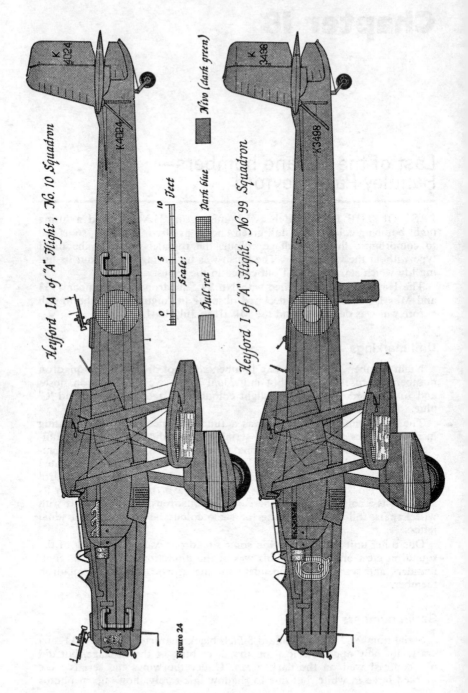

Heyford 1A of "A" Flight, No. 10 Squadron

Heyford 1 of "A" Flight, No 99 Squadron

Scale:

0   5   10   Feet

Dull red

Dark blue

Nivo (dark green)

Figure 24

130

and has given a false impression that they were black. Whereas the serial on the fuselage and rudder was to establish its identity for documentation —servicing records, strength returns, etc—the serial under the wings was for ground reporting purposes, particularly so that the culprit in any breach of flying regulations such as low flying could be identified. For this reason they were marked in white to contrast well.

At times the white serials were given a green washable distemper. Heyfords were frequently used for night air exercises in co-operation with searchlights and the white reflection of the characters under the wings was thought to be too much of a give-away to the ground defences.

The range of numbers allotted to Heyfords is tabled below.

Serial, Mark number and remarks	Known squadron and unit service
J9130 Prototype (New Park No 12, Hendon 1932)	A and AEE
K3489 Non-standard	A and AEE, 149
K3490 I (Disposed in 1939)	99, 7
K3491 I ('T' of 99 Sqn)	99, 7, 97
K3492 I-II ('N' of 99 Sqn)	99, 97
K3493 I ('U' of 99 Sqn)	99, 38, 97
K3494 I (Crashed near Bridlington 1939)	99, 149
K3495 I ('V' of 99 Sqn)	99, 149
K3496 I (Struck off charge, Sept 1939)	99
K3497 I ('W' crashed landing, searchlight exercise)	99
K3498 I ('T' and then 'Q')	99
K3499 I ('X' of 99 Sqn)	99, 38, 97
K3500 I ('R' hit telegraph pole, May 1937)	99
K3501 I (Crashed Nov 11 1936)	99, 38
K3502 I ('M' of 99 Sqn)	99, 149
K3503 I-II-III (New Park No 14, Hendon, 1934)	166
K4021 I-III (Wrecked landing out of fuel, April 1938)	149
K4022 IA (Struck off charge, Aug 29 1939)	10, 97
K4023 IA ('K' of 10 Sqn)	10, 97
K4024 IA ('C' crashed at night, Feb 1936)	10
K4025 IA (Scrapped in 1937)	10, 149
K4026 IA (Undershot Boscombe Down in haze, Oct 1936)	10
K4027 IA ('A' of 10 Sqn)	10, 58
K4028 IA (Scrapped, obsolete 1939)	10, 97
K4029 IA-III (Auto-pilot tests, Oct 1937)	166
K4030 IA (Withdrawn late-1939)	97, 58
K4031 IA	10, 99, 149
K4032 IA ('D' undershot flare path, mid-1938)	10, 149
K4033 IA ('F' of 10 Sqn)	10, 149
K4034 IA (Ditched off Le Havre, Feb 1936)	10, 97
K4035 IA (Wrecked one mile from Boscombe Down)	10
K4036 IA (Disposed in 1937)	99
K4037 IA (Force-landed near Stockton-on-Tees)	10, 149
K4038 IA (Withdrawn mid-1939)	97
K4039 IA (Crashed, Tangmere, Dec 13 1937)	99, 149
K4040 IA (Withdrawn mid-1939)	99, 97
K4041 IA (Withdrawn late-1939)	38, 10, 97, 58
K4042 IA (Struck hillside, Feb 12 1936)	10
K4043 IA (Wing tip flare experiments)	38, 149
K4863 II	7
K4864 II (Crashed, Gainsborough, Dec 12 1936)	102
K4865 II	7, 149
K4866 II ('A' of 7 Sqn)	7, 78, 9, 149
K4867 II	7, 149
K4868 II	102, 78, 7, 97
K4869 II (Crashed edge of airfield, April 28 1936)	7, 97

Serial, Mark number and remarks	Known squadron and unit service
K4870 II	78, 149
K4871 II (Hit trees, Finningley, March 30 1938)	7
K4872 II	102, 78, 7
K4873 II	7
K4874 II (Abandoned due to icing, Dec 12 1936)	102
K4875 II (Withdrawn mid-1939)	7, 149
K4876 II (Hit trees, Finningley, April 6 1937)	7
K4877 II ('H' of 7 Sqn)	97, 7, 99, 149
K4878 II (Withdrawn mid-1939)	97, 7, 99, 149
K5180 III	102, 149
K5181 III	102
K5182 III (Disposed August 1940)	102, 9, 3 AOS
K5183 III (Wrecked, heavy landing, Dec 16 1937)	102
K5184 III (Used for flight refuelling experiments, 1939)	97, 166
K5185 III (Sent to store, April 1939)	10, 9
K5186 III (Delivered to 102 Sqn, July 28 1936)	102
K5187 III (Withdrawn May 18 1940)	102, 149, 4 AOS
K5188 III (Force landed north of York, 1936)	102
K5189 III (Crashed May 1938)	9
K5190 III (Undershot flarepath, Scampton, Sept 1 1937	9
K5191 III (Withdrawn August 20 1940)	99, 149, 148, 3 AOS
K5192 III (To store March 1939)	9
K5193 III (Withdrawn July 20 1940)	10, 102, 4 AOS
K5194 III (Hit trees at Stradishall, Nov 14 1938)	10, 78, 9
K5195 III (Withdrawn mid-1940)	10, 78, 166
K5196 III (Withdrawn mid-1940)	10, 98, 99, 148
K5197 III (Withdrawn mid-1940)	10, 78, 99, 148
K5198 III (Withdrawn mid-1940)	10, 78, 99, 148
K5199 III (Wrecked, wingtip hit tree, Aug 15 1939)	99, 148, 149, 3 AOS
K6857 III (Withdrawn mid-1940)	99, 149, 148, 3 AOS
K6858 III (Struck off charge in March 1938)	99, 149, 99
K6859 III (Withdrawn mid-1940)	99, 102, 149, 4 AOS
K6860 III (Hit stack ½ mile from Everton)	102
K6861 III	
K6862 III (Withdrawn mid-1940)	38, 78, 166, 4 AOS
K6863 III	38, 9, 97, 166
K6864 III (Withdrawn mid-1940)	99, 148, 3 AOS
K6865 III (Crashed on range, Jan 5 1938)	9
K6866 III (Withdrawn mid-1940)	9, 4 AOS
K6867 III (Crashed, engine cut near Scampton, Aug 1937)	9
K6868 III (Withdrawn mid-1940)	9, 4 AOS
K6869 III (Withdrawn mid-1940)	9, 4 AOS
K6870 III (Withdrawn mid-1940)	9, 97, 4 AOS
K6871 III (Withdrawn mid-1940)	38, 99, 149, 3 AOS
K6872 III (Withdrawn mid-1940)	38, 97, 166
K6873 III	7, 97, 166
K6874 III (Used on experimental work, 1940)	7, 97, 166, 102
K6875 III (Hit hill at Edale, July 22 1937)	7, 97, 166
K6876 III (Withdrawn mid-1940)	7, 99, 149, 148
K6877 III	7, 99, 149
K6878 III (Withdrawn mid-1940)	7, 102, 9, 4 AOS
K6879 III	10
K6880 III (Burnt out at Weston, May 29 1937)	166
K6881 III (To store, May 1939)	9
K6882 III (Undercarriage collapsed landing at Scampton, Nov 30 1936	9
K6883 III (Withdrawn March 1940)	9, 4 AOS
K6884 III	
K6885 III (Withdrawn mid-1940)	78, 99, 148, 3 AOS
K6886 III (Scrapped from store in 1939)	78, 166
K6887 III (Withdrawn mid-1940)	166

Serial, Mark number and remarks	Known squadron and unit service
K6888 III (Scrapped in 1941)	166, 4 AOS
K6889 III (Withdrawn mid-1940)	166
K6890 III (Hit hangar, Leconfield, 1939)	166
K6891 III (Withdrawn mid-1940)	166, 4 AOS
K6892 III (Withdrawn mid-1940)	166
K6893 III (Withdrawn mid-1940)	99, 9, 4 AOS
K6894 III	99
K6895 III	166
K6896 III (Withdrawn mid-1940)	102, 148, 4 AOS
K6897 III (Hit hangar, Driffield, April 29 1939)	149, 99, 148, 4 AOS
K6898 III (Force-landed, Disley, Dec 12 1936)	102
K6899 III (Withdrawn mid-1940)	102, 148, 3 AOS
K6900 III (Hit hill, Hebdon Bridge, Dec 13 1936)	102
K6901 III (Scrapped from store in 1939)	102, 149
K6902 III (Used in radar research experiments, 1936-37)	9
K6903 III	149, 99, 9
K6904 III (Withdrawn mid-1940)	149, 9, 3 AOS
K6905 III (Withdrawn mid-1940)	99, 148, 3 AOS
K6906 III (Struck off charge in 1940)	99, 9, 4 AOS

Notes:

A and AEE: Aircraft and Armament Experimental Establishment, AOS: Air Observer School.

Heyfords differed as follows:

Mk I: 2 × Rolls-Royce Kestrel IIIS or IIIS-5 engines.

Mk IA: 2 × Rolls-Royce Kestrel IIIS or IIIS-5 engines with modified engine bearers giving a 200 lb weight saving and a motor-driven generator replaced the wind generator.

Mk II: 2 × Rolls-Royce Kestrel VI (derated) engines.

Mk III: 2 × Rolls-Royce Kestrel VI (full power setting). Steam condensers in leading-edge of top outer planes. Four-bladed propellers replaced initial two-bladed propellers.

Mks I and IA may have been interchanged on repair or reconditioning.

Chapter 19

First of the monoplane bombers—
Fairey Hendon

THE FAIREY HENDON was something of a mystery aircraft. It only fully equipped one squadron, No 38, and it was the only heavy bomber to come from Fairey Aviation. As a monoplane heavy bomber, it represented the height of modernity when it made its first flight in November 1931 at which time it was known as the Fairey Night Bomber.

It was the first, and only, service monoplane to be given the dark green Nivo finish, and correspondingly, it had the blue and red roundels on fuselage sides and well outboard on the upper- and lower-surfaces of the wings. The prototype differed by having large wing roundels, overlapping the ailerons, but the production aircraft, produced after the 1934 ruling that national markings should not overlap control surfaces, had smaller wing roundels.

Manufacture was limited to K1695, the prototype, and 14 production aircraft, K5085-5098, of which every production aircraft saw service in No 38 Squadron; the first arrived at Mildenhall for the squadron on November 20 1936. It has been stated that Hendons also equipped No 115 Squadron, but this is only partly true. No Hendons were officially allotted to No 115 Squadron, which reformed June 15 1937. It was on this date that the 'B' Flight Hendons of No 38 Squadron, then stationed at Marham, were loaned to No 115 Squadron, sharing the station, pending the delivery of their Harrows. Within two months they were back as 'B' Flight No 38 Squadron. During these two months no known change was made to markings, not that either squadron was lavish in this respect.

The only squadron marking was an individual letter, in flight colours, officially red, yellow and blue, for 'A', 'B' and 'C' flights respectively and this was restricted to fuselage sides aft of the roundel. The squadron had three flights of four aircraft with two in reserve. A squadron badge was officially approved in 1937 with the official painting of the crest, 'a heron volant', being presented that August, but there is no record of this being marked on their large gaunt Hendons.

The Hendon was probably the only Nivo-finished aircraft to bear warning markings. On each side of the engines on the wing leading edges the warning notice 'KEEP CLEAR OF AIRSCREWS' was marked in white.

As with the Heyfords, the serial numbers of the Hendons on the rear fuselage in black 8-inch characters tended to become 'lost' against the mas-

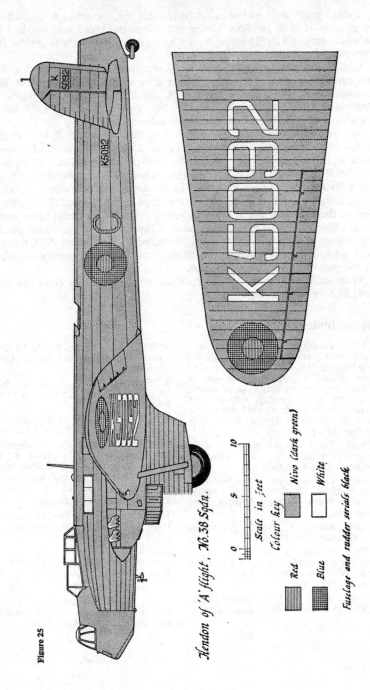

Figure 25

Hendon of 'A' flight, No. 38 Sqdn.

Scale in feet

0   5   10

Colour key

| | Red | | Nivo (dark green) |
| | Blue | | White |

Fuselage and rudder serials black

sive dark green bulk of the aircraft. On the tail, the serial was marked on both sides of both rudders. Under the wings the serial was marked large in white, until mid-1938 when it was washed over in green to render it less conspicuous.

Unlike day bombers, Hendons were unaffected by the Munich crisis in the summer of 1938, their dark green scheme being considered sufficient as camouflage. On November 24 1938, the first of the No 38 Squadron's Wellingtons, L4230, arrived and by the second week of 1939 the last Hendon had been withdrawn from squadron service.

Although every aircraft was needed at this period of RAF expansion it was not a practical proposition to keep a single squadron of non-standard aircraft functioning, particularly as their top speed of 150 mph with a 1,660 lb bomb load would make them exceedingly vulnerable. An order for a further 60 had been cancelled in favour of more modern aircraft. On investigation, it was decided that these large aircraft, similar in configuration to the Harrows and Whitleys coming into service, could serve usefully at the Electrical and Wireless School, Cranwell, giving trainees practical experience in wiring. After war was declared in September 1939, there was such an intake of trainees that eventually ten Hendons were re-numbered in the instructional airframe series.

With such small numbers of Hendons, space permits a complete individual history of each one:

Serial history

K1695 Prototype delivered to Aircraft and Armament Experimental Establishment on May 8 1932, then to Nos 10 and 9 Squadrons for service trials. No unit markings borne except black No 13 on fuselage side as New Type Park Number at 1932 RAF Display at Hendon. Disposed in September 1938.

K5085 Used on development work before reaching No 38 Squadron. Became 1614M at Cranwell.

K5086 Delivered in September 1936 and became 'E' of No 38 Squadron, then 1564M after leaving the squadron.

K5087 Served in No 38 Squadron before becoming 1565M.

K5088 Served in No 38 Squadron and became 1615M at No 1 Electrical and Wireless School, Cranwell, in August 1939.

K5089 'K' of No 38 Squadron joined K5088 at Cranwell in August 1939.

K5090 After service in No 38 Squadron was stored at the Home Aircraft Depot.

K5091 After a year's service in No 38 Squadron was wrecked in December 1937.

K5092 'C' of No 38 Squadron; this aircraft became 1617M at Cranwell.

K5093 Served in No 38 Squadron, and became 1566M after a short period in No 10 Maintenance Unit.

K5094 Served in No 38 Squadron from December 1936 to December 1938 when it was scrapped.

K5095 Served in No 38 Squadron from January 1937 to November 1938 when it was scrapped.

K5096 Served in No 38 Squadron and became 1618M at Cranwell.

K5097 Served in No 38 Squadron and became 1619M at Cranwell.

K5098 Last Hendon built, delivered March 1 1937 to No 38 Squadron and became 1567M in 1939.

79 *No 45 Squadron IIIFs at Helwan, Egypt, 1930. The aircraft are numbered clockwise on their fins—No 12 being on the extreme right—and the number is repeated in white on the top of the rear fuselage decking.*

80 *No 47 Squadron's Gordons were at times fitted with floats for operating from the Nile. This aircraft, J9161, bears an 'R' in its serial to denote that it has been rebuilt* (Ministry of Defence H730).

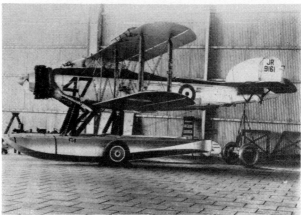

81 *Another rebuilt Gordon of No 47 Squadron shown before rudder striping was abolished in 1934* (Ministry of Defence H736).

82 *The Gordon II shown above had revised control surfaces. Most were delivered to store as a reserve, like this example bereft of squadron markings.* 83 *Gordon I on the left is shown during service in No 35 Squadron which was from September 1935 to October 1937 (C. E. Sargeant).*

84 (Above) The prototype Hawker Hart photographed on September 25 1929 (Ministry of Defence 6086).
85 (Left) A Hawker Hart in operational service in India with No 11 Squadron which used fuselage bands to identify its aircraft (via E. B. Goldsmith).

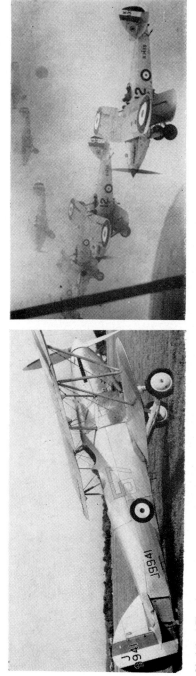

87 (Above) Aircraft of 'Shiny Twelve' in a murky sky which nevertheless shows the positioning of the unit number by the gunner's cockpit, and the size of the disc containing the foxhead insignia on the fin.

88 (Left) The unusually large presentation of the badge on the fin and a dark green fuselage decking characterised No 605 Squadron's Harts. Comparing this picture with photo No 87 it will be seen that, when rudder stripes were deleted, wing roundels became smaller, the point being that the 1934 order which effected this was concerned with removing all paintwork from control surfaces, ailerons as well as rudders.

86 (Above) The sole surviving Hart, originally a civil demonstration aircraft G-ABMR, was marked up as J9933 in 1959 and later re-marked as shown to represent an aircraft of No 57 Squadron.

Chapter 20

Towards a new era in markings

THE MARKINGS of bomber aircraft is not a subject that can be covered in complete isolation. Regulations on the markings of aircraft between the wars were issued by the Air Ministry as applicable to all aircraft, and the only division recognised was in day flying and night flying aircraft. In effect, since only the heavy bomber units were trained as night flying units, this made a division for markings of the heavy bombers on the one hand, and all other classes of aircraft on the other. Thus many of the general marking regulations quoted in the preceding chapters for the day bombers also covered the majority of aircraft in the RAF, and those general regulations given for heavy bombers were exclusive to aircraft operating in that role.

In retrospect

To recap in broad terms, for most of the years between the wars, RAF aircraft were of two shades—a silver (aluminium) finish for all aircraft including day bombers, and a dark green (Nivo) finish for night bombers.

Until 1936, squadrons both at home and overseas were grouped under various commands that included in some cases both bomber and fighter elements. A Bomber Command was not formed until July 14 1936 with Nos 1, 2 and 3 Groups and auxiliary units placed temporarily in a No 6 Group; Nos 4 and 5 Groups formed on April 1 and September 1 of 1937 by taking over squadrons from an expanding No 3 Group, and the pattern was set for the war which followed.

Up to 1937 only the heavy bombers, with their marking category of night flying aircraft, had been in drab colours. This had been traditional since the First World War when Nivo had been introduced, and continued for two good reasons: firstly, there were no heavy bombers stationed overseas where an aluminium heat-reflecting finish was desirable and, secondly, it implied an operational readiness to retaliate by the bombers stationed in the United Kingdom.

Standardisation

Apart from the overall finishes, there were a series of directives that affected the more detailed markings of aircraft. These are summed up with precise dates in the chronology in Appendix VI.

One item of equipment introduced and issued to units in mid-1931 that influenced standardisation of serial number markings was two sets of stencils. These were known in the official nomenclature as 'Plates, Stencil, Brass, Sets Nos 1 and 2'. The No 1 set was for use in marking part numbers and doping scheme codes in ¼-inch characters; the No 2 set was for use in marking serial numbers in 8-inch characters. This set the standard sizing for these markings that continued throughout the Second World War and remains the same today.

Preservation

The constant striving to preserve aircraft materials has now culminated in complete plastic coverings with polyurethane paints. In the years between the wars, the stage had been reached in the 1920s of anodizing duralumin parts and stove-enamelling over other metal parts. This had the effect of dulling the natural aluminium alloy metals such as duralumin, and stoving colours were limited to black, white and grey as detailed in the Appendices.

Shades of change

For overall finishes the wind of change—perhaps shades of change are more appropriate in this context—came in the 1930s. It was in 1933 that the Nazis came to power and, following revelations of the existence of a German Air Force (the *Luftwaffe* actually had a numerical strength of 1,888 aircraft in December 1934), an RAF Expansion Programme was started. With the realisation that our own airfields could become targets and that the constitution of a field force operating again from the continent could become a necessity, general camouflage was introduced.

From 1934 onwards there was experimentation in suitable shades with a Westland Wapiti as a test aircraft to represent all operational aircraft. Finally in 1936 a shadow scheme with a disruptive pattern of dark green and dark earth was introduced, effective on all production aircraft from April 1937. So that, while the prototypes of the Blenheim, Whitley, Hampden, and Wellington all appeared in aluminium finishes, every production aircraft of these types was in camouflage.

For the new bomber transport, the Bristol Bombay, a monoplane transport to replace the ageing Valentias, the change came on the production line. The first 11, L5808 to L5818, were delivered in silver, and the 12th aircraft, L5919, and all subsequent were delivered in camouflage.

Since the camouflage finishes introduced in 1937 remained in force for some years and set the pattern for camouflage schemes for the Second World War, 1937 is a very suitable point to finish the first volume of *Bombing Colours*.

APPENDIX I: British aircraft serial ranges, 1912-37

Serial range	Service	Years covered	Aircraft concerned
1-200	Royal Naval Air Service	1912-14	General naval allocation
201-800	Royal Flying Corps	1912-14	General military allocation
801-1600	Royal Naval Air Service	1914-15	General naval allocation
1601-3000	Royal Flying Corps	1914-15	General military allocation
3001-4000	Royal Naval Air Service	1915	General naval allocation
4001-5000	Royal Flying Corps	1915	General military allocation
5001-5200	Royal Flying Corps	1915	Purchases from French industry
5201-8000	Royal Flying Corps	1915-16	General military allocation
8001-10000	Royal Naval Air Service	1916	General naval allocation
A1-115	Royal Flying Corps	1916	Originally allotted to Royal Aircraft Factory but some later sub-contracted
A116-315	Royal Flying Corps in the Field	1916	Purchases from French industry
A316-5799	Royal Flying Corps	1916	General military allocation
A5800-5899	—	—	Not allotted
A5900-6600	Royal Flying Corps	1916	General military allocation
A6601-6800	Royal Flying Corps in the Field	1916	Purchases from French industry
A6801-9999	Royal Flying Corps	1916	General military allocation
B1-700	Royal Flying Corps	1916	General military allocation
B701-900	Royal Flying Corps	1916-17	Rebuilt from salvage at No 1 (Southern) Aircraft Repair Depot, South Farnborough
B901-1500	Royal Flying Corps	1916-17	General military allocation
B1501-1700	Royal Flying Corps in the Field	1916-17	Purchases from French industry
B1701-3450	Royal Flying Corps	1917	General military allocation
B3451-3650	Royal Flying Corps in the Field	1917	Purchases from French industry
B3651-4000	Royal Flying Corps	1917	Miscellaneous acquisitions including re-numbered aircraft
B4001-4200	Royal Flying Corps	1917-18	Rebuilt from salvage at No 2 (Northern) Aircraft Repair Depot, Coal Aston
B4201-6730	Royal Flying Corps	1917	General military allocation
B6731-7130	Royal Flying Corps	1917	Purchases from French industry
B7131-7730	Royal Flying Corps	1917	General military allocation
B7731-8230	Royal Flying Corps	1917-18	Rebuilt from salvage at No 1 (Southern) Aircraft Repair Depot, South Farnborough
B8231-8830	Royal Flying Corps	1917	General and miscellaneous allocation
B8831-9030	Royal Flying Corps	1917-18	Rebuilt from salvage at No 3 (Western) Aircraft Repair Depot, Yate
B9031-9999	Royal Flying Corps	1917-18	General military and miscellaneous acquisitions
C1-9985	Royal Flying Corps	1917	General military acquisitions
C9986-9999	Royal Flying Corps	1917	Rebuilt from salvage by training units
D1-4960	Royal Flying Corps	1917-18	General military allocation

Serial range	Service	Years covered	Aircraft concerned
D4961-5000	Royal Flying Corps	1917-18	Rebuilt from salvage at No 3 (Western) Aircraft Repair Depot, Yate
D5001-9999	Royal Flying Corps	1918	General military allocation
E1-1600	Royal Flying Corps	1918	General military allocation
E1601-9956	Royal Air Force	1918	General military allocation
E9957-9983	Royal Air Force	1918	Rebuilt from salvage at No 3 (Western) Aircraft Repair Depot under emergency arrangements
E9984-9999	Royal Air Force	1918	Rebuilt and miscellaneous acquisitions
F1-320	Royal Air Force	1918	General military allocation
F321-350	Royal Air Force	1918	Reservation for No 2 (Northern) Aircraft Repair Depot
F351-615	Royal Air Force	1918	General military allocation
F616-700	Royal Air Force	1918	Further reservation to No 2 (Northern) Aircraft Repair Depot
F701-2182	Royal Air Force	1918	General military allocation
F2183-2232	Royal Air Force	1918	Rebuilds and miscellaneous acquisitions
F2233-4170	Royal Air Force	1918	General military allocation
F4171-4220	Royal Air Force	1918	Built up from salvage
F4221-5800	Royal Air Force	1918	General military allocation
F5801-6300	Royal Air Force	1918	Rebuilt from salvage by depots in France
F6301-8200	Royal Air Force	1918	General military allocation
F8201-8420	Royal Air Force	1918	Cancelled orders
F8421-9295	Royal Air Force	1918	General military allocation
F9296-9495	Royal Air Force	1918	Reservations and cancelled orders
F9496-9545	Royal Air Force	1918-19	Rebuilt from salvage by No 5 (Eastern) Aircraft Repair Depot, Henlow
F9546-9572	Royal Air Force	1918	Replacements, reservations and miscellaneous acquisitions
F9573-9622	Royal Air Force	1918	Reservation for No 3 (Western) Aircraft Repair Depot, Yate
F9623-9638	Royal Air Force	1918	Rebuilt from salvage at units in the UK
F9639-9694	Royal Air Force	1918	Reservation for No 2 (Northern) Aircraft Repair Depot, Coal Aston
F9695-9995	Royal Air Force	1918	General military allocation
F9996-9999	Royal Air Force	1918	Reservation for No 2 (Northern) Aircraft Repair Depot
G	RNAS, RFC and RAF	1917-18	Reserved as prefix to register wrecked or captured German aircraft
H1-6842	Royal Air Force	1918	General military allocation
H6843-7342	Royal Air Force	1918-19	Rebuilt from salvage by Depots in France
H7343-8112	Royal Air Force	1918	General military allocation
H8113-8252	Royal Air Force	1918	Reservation for No 2 (Northern) Aircraft Repair Depot

APPENDIX I

Serial range	Service	Years covered	Aircraft concerned
H8253-8412	Royal Air Force	1918	Rebuilds and miscellaneous acquisitions
H8413-9966	Royal Air Force	1918	General military allocation
H9967-9999	Royal Air Force	1918	Reservation
J1-4591	Royal Air Force	1918	General military allocation of which the majority were cancelled due to Armistice
J4592-5091	Royal Air Force	1918	Reserved for rebuilds from salvage by Depots in France but not subscribed due to Armistice
J5092-6572	Royal Air Force	1918	General military allocation of which majority were cancelled due to Armistice
J6573-6585	Royal Air Force	1919	Post-war experimentals
J6586-9999	Royal Air Force	1919-29	Post-war production and prototypes
K1-99	—	—	Not used
K100-999	—	1919	Allocation for register of civil aircraft subscribed up to K175 before registration letters were adopted
K1000-9999	Royal Air Force	1929-36	Production and prototypes
L1000-7272	Royal Air Force	1936-37	Production and prototypes. Up to this point numbers taken up consecutively
L7273-9999	Royal Air Force	1937	Production and prototypes. From this point blocks of up to 50 numbers omitted as security measure
M	Royal Air Force	1921-72	Used only as a suffix on aircraft recorded as ground instructional airframes
N1-100	Royal Naval Air Service	1916-18	Experimental seaplanes
N101-499	Royal Air Force	1918-27	Experimental marine aircraft. Not used after N255 except for N300
N500-999	Royal Naval Air Service	1916-17	Naval experimental landplanes. Used up to N546
N1000-2999	Royal Naval Air Service	1916-18	Naval production floatplanes and light flying boats
N3000-3999	Royal Naval Air Service	1916-18	Reservation, and partly subscribed by landplane purchases from France
N4000-4999	Royal Naval Air Service and Royal Air Force	1916-18	Production large flying boats
N5000-8230	Royal Naval Air Service and Royal Air Force	1916-18	Production naval landplanes
N8231-8999	Royal Air Force	1918	Reservation, not taken up due to Armistice
N9000-9449	Royal Air Force	1918	Production seaplanes
N9500-9999	Royal Air Force	1919-25	Production marine aircraft
N1000-9999	Royal Air Force	1937-38	Second series of N prefix continuing on from L9999. Subsequent P and R ranges outside scope of book
S1000-1865	Royal Air Force and Fleet Air Arm	1925-32	Marine aircraft following on from N9999 (first series)
X1-25	Ministry of Munitions	1917-18	Licence register for private ventures.

APPENDIX II: Colouring and finishes of British bombers between the Wars

Official Stores designation	Official description	Application to bomber aircraft	Representative current standard for application to replica or model aircraft to achieve authenticity
33A/57	Black enamel, air drying	Protection of wood and timber, night bombers	Any good black paint
33A/58	Dark green enamel	Identification of pipe-lines	Current commercial enamel to same shade as official description
33A/59	Light green enamel	Identification of pipe-lines	Any light green
33A/60	White enamel, air drying	Protection of metal and timber, day bombers	White
33A/62	Grey enamel, air drying	Protection of metal and timber, day bombers	Battleship grey
33A/104	Black anti-sulphuric acid paint	Accumulator boxes	Any good black paint
33A/196	Pale opal varnish	Interior woodwork	Any current pale opal varnish
33A/197	Pale opal varnish	Interior woodwork	Any current pale opal varnish
33A/332	Black stoving enamel	Metal parts, one coat, brushed or sprayed	Black enamel
33A/333	Black stoving enamel	Metal parts, two coats, brushed or dipped	Black enamel
33A/341	Bright blue enamel, air drying	Identification of water pipe-lines	Not applicable to models. Commercial paint for replicas
33A/342	Scarlet enamel, air drying	Identification of petrol pipe-lines	Current commercial enamel to same shade as official description
33A/343	Yellow enamel, air drying	Identification of compressed air pipes	Current commercial enamel to same shade as official description
33B/1	Seaplane varnish	External woodwork and metal fittings	Light grey finish

146

Ref	Description	Application	Notes
33B/2	Dull red identification colour	Roundel centres on night bombers	Terra cotta
33B/3	Bright blue identification colour	Roundel outers on day bombers	Commercial model paints marketed as glossy roundel blue Similar to Humbrol Signal Red
33B/4	Bright red identification colour	Roundel centres on day bombers	There is only one true shade of white
33B/5	White identification colour	Roundel inners on day bombers	
33B/6	Dull blue identification colour	Roundel outers on night bombers	Matt dark blue
33B/7	Aluminium covering dope	Overall finish day bombers	Similar appearance obtained by Airfix G8 or Humbrol HB14 on plastic models
33B/9	Nivo	Overall finish for night bombers	Dull green finish but with faint sheen
33B/17	Battleship grey, flat	Cowlings up to mid-1920s	Similar to Ocean Grey Airfix M2, Humbrol HB3 or Model-colour RA3
33B/23	Matt black identification colour	Serial, part and dope scheme markings	Any commercial matt black paint
33B/26	Transparent dope	Covering dope for identification colours on day bombers	Clear dope such as Joyplane
33B/35	White paint, dope resisting	For use with protectives in contact with doped parts	Commercial white paint for model. Consult Cellon for replicas
33B/36	ADP pigmented dope	Overall finish day bombers in UK. Withdrawn 1932	Aluminium paint
33B/37	ADPT tropical use pigmented dope	Overall finish day bombers overseas. Withdrawn 1932	Aluminium paint
33B/38	Aluminium paint	Final coat — Fabric covered wooden parts and in bolt holes of wooden airscrews	Alminium paint
33B/40	Grey undercoating paint	Initial coat — in bolt holes of wooden airscrews	Grey undercoat. Precise shade not important since covered

Official Stores designation	Official description	Application to bomber aircraft	Representative current standard for application to replica or model aircraft to achieve authenticity
33B/50	Cellulose enamel, Engine No 1	Brushed } External preservation	Commercial cellulose enamel
33B/51	Cellulose enamel, Engine No 2	Sprayed } of engine parts	Commercial cellulose enamel
33B/52	Cellulose lacquer	Undercoat for wooden propellers	Commercial cellulose lacquer
33B/53	Cellulose lacquer	Finishing application for propellers	Commercial cellulose lacquer
33B/54	Cellulose enamel, cockpits	Cockpits of all aircraft	Commercial cellulose enamel
33B/55	Cellulose enamel, marine	Final coating on parts applicable to 33B/63	Commercial cellulose enamel
33B/63	White enamel undercoating	Metal (except stainless steel) floats	Commercial white
33B/65 and 66	Black matt identification covering	Serial and part numbers marked over aluminium doping	Commercial matt black
33B/67 and 68	Bright blue identification covering	Roundel outers on day bombers	Commercial model paints marketed as glossy roundel blue
33B/69 and 70	Dull blue identification covering	Roundel outers on night bombers in Nivo	Matt dark blue
33B/71 and 72	Bright red identification covering	Roundel centres on day bombers in aluminium	Similar to Humbrol Signal Red
33B/73 and 74	Dull red identification covering	Roundel centres on night bombers in Nivo	Terra cotta
33B/75 and 76	White identification covering	Roundel inners on day bombers in aluminium	Commercial white
33B/77 and 78	Yellow identification covering	Flight and individual letter markings	Airfix M15, Humbrol 24 or Modelcolor RA9
33B/85-87	Transparent covering	Roundel and rudder striping final application, day bombers	Clear dope such as Joyplane

148

33B/118-120	Aluminium dopes	Cellon and Titanine overall 'silver' finish for day bombers	Similar appearance obtained by Airfix G8 or Humbrol HB14 on plastic models
33B/121-123	Nivo dopes	General overall finish for night bombers	Dull green finish but with faint sheen
33B/124-126	Red dope	Initial doping of all fabric, two coats	Undercoat not applicable to models

Notes:

The official stores reference is in the RAF Stores Vocabulary in which 33 relates to the class of store, in this case dopes, paints and varnishes, and the A and B a division within that class. The individual numbers were allotted for paints varnishes to a particular specification added to the range. Numbers omitted have been those without direct reference to conditioning markings, for example 33B/8 was a dope brush wash and 33B/11 a varnish remover.

It will be seen that the colours repeat themselves; this is due to a revision of doping schemes in 1931 when a change was made to standardise on Cellon CX and Titanine T2S finishing schemes. This did not affect the actual appearance but concerned mainly dope tautening properties and the number and sequence of doping and covering coats.

Where two or more reference numbers have been given for the one item, eg, 33B/121-123, it is due to different capacity containers, 33B/121 was a ¼-gallon tin, 33B/122 a gallon tin and 33B/123 a 5-gallon drum of the same Nivo finishing dope. It was not thought necessary to specify these differences as they in no way condition shades.

Where the application is given for day bombers it may be taken that the finish also applied generally to fighter, general purpose, transport and army co-operation aircraft; but where the application is given for night bombers it may be taken to be exclusively for aircraft in that role which, readers are reminded, had no bright colours and no white roundel inners.

For the official description, the correct names have been used, but in the reverse of the official nomenclature to make it more readable.

Prior to the introduction of the stores classification system, paints and varnishes were identified by a specification number series prefixed by letters V and X, with a letter code for pigments and series of codes for doping schemes; pigment codes are given in Chapter 8.

APPENDIX III: Characteristics of British bombers, 1914-37

Type	Design Organisation	Years of service as bomber	Crew	Span top wing	Length	Engine	Maximum speed/ht (mph/ft)	Service ceiling (ft)	Representative bomb load	Defensive armament
504	Avro	1914-15	1-2	36' 0"	29' 5"	1 × 80 hp Gnome	81/1000	7000	4 × 20 lb	Personal arms
RE5	RAF Farnborough*	1914-15	2	42' 0"	30' 0"	1 × 120 hp Beardmore	78/1000	8000	3 × 20 lb	Personal arms
RE7	RAF Farnborough*	1914-15	2	57' 0"	31' 11"	1 × 150 hp RAF4a	73/5000	14000	1 × 336 lb	1 Lewis m/g
BE2c	RAF Farnborough*	1915-17	1-2	37' 0"	27' 3"	1 × 90 hp RAF1a	72/5000	12000	2 × 112 lb	1 Lewis m/g
Bomber	Short Bros	1915-17	2	85' 0"	45' 0"	1 × 225 hp Sunbeam	77/6500	9500	4 × 230 lb	1 Lewis m/g
BE12	RAF Farnborough*	1916-17	1	37' 0"	27' 3"	1 × 150 hp RAF4a	97/6500	14000	2 × 112 lb	1 Vickers m/g
1½ Strutter	Sopwith	1916-17	2	33' 6"	25' 3"	1 × 130 hp Clerget	98/10000	13000	4 × 56 lb	1 Vickers m/g
1½ Strutter	Sopwith	1916-17	2	33' 6"	25' 3"	1 × 130 hp Clerget	97/10000	15000	12 le Pecq	1 Vickers, 1 Lewis m/gs
FE2b	RAF Farnborough*	1916-18	2	47' 9"	32' 3"	1 × 160 hp Beardmore	72/10000	11000	1 × 230 lb	1 Lewis m/g
0/100	Handley Page	1916-18	4-5	100' 9"	62' 10"	2 × 250 hp R-R Eagles	75/8000	7000	16 × 112 lb	3 Lewis m/gs
FE2d	RAF Farnborough*	1917-18	2	47' 9"	32' 3"	1 × 250 hp R-R Eagle	88/10000	17500	6 × 25 lb	2 Lewis m/gs
DH4	Airco	1917-18	2	42' 5"	30' 8"	1 × 250 hp R-R Eagle	119/3000	16000	2 × 230 lb	Vickers, 1 or 2 Lewis m/gs
DH6	Airco	1917-18	1-2	35' 11"	27' 3"	1 × 90 hp RAF1a	70/1000	7000	1 × 100 lb	Nil
0/400	Handley Page	1917-21	5	100' 0"	62' 0"	2 × 360 hp R-R Eagles	84/6500	8000	3 × 550 lb	Up to 5 Lewis m/gs
Kangaroo	Blackburn	1918	3-4	74' 10"	44' 2"	2 × 250 hp R-R Falcons	98/6500	10500	4 × 230 lb	2 Lewis mg/s
DH9	Airco	1918-19	2	42' 5"	30' 6"	1 × 230 hp BHP	111/10000	17500	2 × 230 lb	1 Vickers, 1 or 2 Lewis m/gs
V/1500	Handley Page	1918-21	6	126' 0"	64' 0"	4 × 375 hp R-R Eagles	98/10000	11000	28 × 250 lb	Up to 6 Lewis m/gs
DH9A	Airco	1918-33	2	46' 0"	30' 2"	1 × 400 hp Liberty 12	114/10000	16500	4 × 100 lb	1 Vickers, 1 Lewis m/g
DH10A	Airco	1918-23	3	65' 6"	39' 8"	2 × 400 hp Liberty 12s	115/10000	20000	8 × 100 lb	Up to 4 Lewis m/gs
Vimy IV	Vickers	1918-33	3	68' 1"	43' 6"	2 × 360 hp R-R Eagles	96/10000	14000	18 × 112 lb	4 Lewis m/gs
Vernon	Vickers	1922-27	3	68' 1"	42' 8"	2 × 450 hp Napier Lions	118/5000	9500	3 × 250 lb	Nil
Aldershot	Avro	1924-26	3	68' 0"	45' 0"	1 × 650 hp R-R Condor III	111/10000	11500	3 × 250 lb	1 Lewis m/g
Fawn II	Fairey	1924-33	2	49' 11"	32' 1"	1 × 450 hp Napier Lion	107/10000	13875	4 × 112 lb	1 Vickers, 1 Lewis m/gs
Virginia VII	Vickers	1924-29	4	86' 6"	50' 7"	2 × 500 hp Napier Lions	104/10000	8000	14 × 112 lb	3 Lewis m/gs

Name	Manufacturer	Crew	Years	Wingspan	Length	Engine	Speed/Alt	Ceiling	Bomb load	Armament
Victoria V	Vickers	2	1926-38	87' 4"	59' 6"	2 × 570 hp Napier Lions	112/10000	18500	4 × 112 lb	Nil
Horsley	Hawker	2	1926-34	56' 6"	38' 10"	1 × 650 hp R-R Condor	112/10000	14000	2 × 250 lb	1 Vickers, 1 Lewis m/g
Fox	Fairey	2	1926-31	38' 0"	31' 2"	1 × 480 hp Curtiss D12	150/10000	17000	4 × 112 lb	1 Vickers, 1 Lewis m/g
Hyderabad	Handley Page	4	1926-34	75' 0"	59' 2"	2 × 450 hp Napier Lions	112/10000	14000	4 × 250 lb	3 Lewis m/gs
Virginia IX	Vickers	4	1927-33	87' 8"	62' 3"	2 × 580 hp Napier Lions	109/5000	15500	14 × 112 lb	3 Lewis m/gs
IIIF	Fairey	2	1927-40	45' 9"	36' 9"	1 × 570 hp Napier Lion	120/10000	20000	4 × 112 lb	1 Vickers, 1 Lewis m/g
Wapiti	Westland	2	1928-38	46' 5"	32' 6"	1 × 550 hp Bristol Jupiter	134/10000	20500	4 × 112 lb	1 Vickers, 1 Lewis m/g
Sidestrand III	Boulton & Paul	4-5	1928-38	71' 11"	46' 0"	2 × 460 hp Bristol Jupiters	140/10000	10500	4 × 250 lb	3 Lewis m/gs
Hinaidi II	Handley Page	4	1929-37	75' 0"	59' 2"	2 × 440 hp Bristol Jupiters	115/10000	14500	12 × 112 lb	3 Lewis m/gs
Hart	Hawker	2	1930-42	37' 4"	27' 4"	1 × 525 hp R-R Kestrel	170/10000	21250	10 × 50 lb	1 Vickers, 1 Lewis m/g
Gordon	Fairey	2	1931-37	45' 9"	36' 9"	1 × 525 hp A-S Panther	147/10000	22000	4 × 100 lb	1 Vickers, 1 Lewis m/g
Heyford	Handley Page	4	1933-39	75' 0"	58' 0"	2 × 525 hp R-R Kestrels	142/13000	21000	28 × 100 lb	3 Lewis m/gs
Wallace	Westland	2	1933-39	46' 5"	34' 2"	1 × 680 hp Bristol Pegasus	158/15000	24000	4 × 112 lb	1 Vickers, 1 Lewis m/g
Overstrand	Boulton & Paul	3-5	1934-41	72' 0"	46' 0"	2 × 580 hp Bristol Pegasus	153/6500	22500	6 × 250 lb	3 Lewis m/gs
Valentia	Vickers	2	1934-42	87' 4"	59' 6"	2 × 635 hp Bristol Pegasus	120/5000	16250	8 × 250 lb	2 Lewis m/gs from 1936
Vincent	Vickers	3	1934-38	49' 0"	36' 8"	1 × 635 hp Bristol Pegasus	143/5000	19000	8 × 112 lb	1 Vickers, 1 Lewis m/g
Hind	Hawker	2	1935-39	37' 3"	29' 3"	1 × 640 hp R-R Kestrel	184/15000	26500	4 × 112 lb	1 Vickers, 1 Lewis m/g
Hendon II	Fairey	5	1936-39	101' 9"	60' 9"	2 × 600 hp R-R Kestrels	150/10000	21500	6 × 250 lb	3 Lewis m/gs

* RAF in this case is the Royal Aircraft Factory.

APPENDIX IV: Airframe serial numbers of British aircraft types used as bombers or bomber trainers, 1914-37

Where production was by other than the design firm or establishment, the short name of the manufacturer is given in brackets and only to the range of numbers within the punctuation, the full name and address of the manufacturer is given in Appendix V.

Avro 504: 179, 383, 398, 568, 637, 683, 715, 750-793, 873-878, 2857-2860, 4221-4225, 4255.

Avro 504A: 2890-2939, 4020-4069, 4737-4786, 7716-7740 (all subsequent 504As built for training purposes only).

Avro 504B: 1001-1050, 9821-9830, 9861-9890 (Parnall), N5250-5279 (Sunbeam), N5310-5329 (British Caudron), N5800-5829 and N6010-6029 (Parnall), N6130-6159 (Sunbeam), N6650-6679.

Avro 504C: 1467-1496 and 3301-3320 (Brush Electrical), 8574-8603.

Avro 523 Pike: Two un-numbered experimental bombers.

Avro 533 Manchester: F3492 Mk II, F3493 Mk I, F3494 Mk III not completed.

Avro 549 Aldershot: J6852-6853 prototypes, J6942-6956.

Avro 557 Ava: N171-172, long range coastal defence or night bomber.

Avro 604 Antelope: J9183, experimental high performance day bomber.

BE2a: 217-218, 220, 222 and 225-242 (Bristol), 249-250, 267, 272-273, 276, 298-299, 303, 314, 316-318, 320-321, 327-336, 340, 347-349, 368, 372, 385-386, 407, 441-442, 447, 449, 452-454 (Vickers), 457, 465-466, 468-481, 483-488, 601, 667.

BE2b: 396-397 (Bristol), 492-493, 646, 650, 666, 687, 705, 709, 746, 2175-2180 and 2770-2819 (Jonques) of which late deliveries were as BE2c, 2884-2889 (Whitehead) produced too late for operational use.

BE2c: 952-963 (Vickers), 964-975 (Blackburn), 976-987 (Hewlett & Blondeau), 988-999 (Martinsyde), 1075-1098 (Vickers), 1099-1122 (Beardmore), 1123-1146 (Blackburn), 1147-1170 (Grahame-White), 1183-1188 (Eastbourne Aviation), 1189-1194 (Hewlett & Blondeau), 1652-1747 (Bristol), 1748-1779 (Vickers), 1780-1800 and 2000-2029 (Armstrong Whitworth), 2030-2129 (Daimler), 2470-2569 (Wolseley) of which some were completed as BE2d or BE2e, 2570-2669 (Daimler), 2670-2769 (Ruston Proctor), 3999 (Blackburn), 4070-4219 (Bristol), 4300-4599 (G & J Weir), 4700-4709 built as single-seaters, 4710-4725 (Vickers at Crayford), 5384-5403 (Wolseley), 5413-5441 and 7321-7345 (Vickers), 8293-8304 (Grahame-White), 8326-8337 (Beardmore), 8404-8409 (Eastbourne Aviation), 8410-8433 (Hewlett & Blondeau), 8488-8500 (Beardmore), 8606-8629 (Blackburn), 8714-8724 (Beardmore), 9456-9475 transferred to RNAS from RFC, 9951-10000 (Blackburn).

BE2d: 5730-5879 (Bristol), 6228-6327 (Ruston Proctor), 6728-6827 (Vulcan Motor & Engineering), 7058-7257 (Bristol). Many of these aircraft ordered as BE2d were actually delivered as BE2e.

BE2c/e: Numbers of BE2c airframes under construction in 1916-17 were completed as BE2es; in general, the early numbers of each of the following batches were BE2cs and the later numbers BE2es, A1261-1310 (Barclay Curle), A1311-1360 (Napier & Miller), A1361-1410 (Denny Bros),

A1792-1891 (Vulcan Motor & Engineering), A3049-3168 (Wolseley), B6151-6200 (British Caudron at Alloa).

BE2e: A2733-2982 and A8626-8725 (Bristol), B3651-3750 (Vulcan Motor & Engineering), B4401-4600 (Bristol), C6901-7000 (Denny Bros), C7001-7100 (Barclay Curle), C7101-7200 (Napier & Miller).

Blackburn Beagle: N236 high altitude experimental bomber.

Blackburn Cubaroo: N166-167 experimental bomber.

Blackburn GP: 1415 experimental maritime patrol bomber.

Blackburn Kangaroo: B8837-8840, B9970-9989 maritime bomber.

Blackburn SP: 1416 experimental maritime patrol bomber.

Beardmore WB1: N525 experimental long-range bomber.

Boulton & Paul Bourges: Experimental twin-engined bomber, F2903 Mk I, F2904 Mk IA, F2905 Mk II.

Boulton & Paul Bugle: Limited production medium-range bomber that did not go into service, J6984-6985, J7235, J7259, J7260, J7266-7267.

Boulton & Paul Overstrand: J9185-9186 prototypes converted from Sidestrand airframes plus J9179 also converted, K4546-4564, K8173-8177.

Boulton & Paul P32: Experimental J9950.

Boulton & Paul Sidestrand: J7938-7939 prototypes that went into squadron service as Mk I. For production aircraft detail, see listing in Chapter 14.

Bristol Berkeley: J7403-7405 day or night bomber prototypes.

Bristol Braemar: C4296 Mk I, C4297 Mk II prototypes.

Caudron GIV: 3289-3300 French-built, 3333-3344 (British Caudron Co), 3894-3899 French-built, 9101-9131 French-built.

Note in the de Havilland designs following, the manufacturer is, unless otherwise given in brackets within the punctuation, the Aircraft Manufacturing Company of Hendon, London.

DH3: 7744 day bomber prototype.

DH4: 3696 prototype re-numbered later B394, A2125-2174, A7401-8089, B2051-2150 (Berwick), B1482, B3955-3968, B3987, B5451-5550 (Vulcan Motor & Engineering), B9434-9439, B9470-9471 and B9994 built up from spares, C4501-4540, D1751-1775 (Westland), D8351-8430, D9231-9280, E4624-4628, F1551-1552, F2633-2732 (Glendower), F5699-5798 (Palladium Autocars), F7597-9598, H5290 (Glendower), H5894-5939 and H8263 (Palladium Autocars). Additionally F5809, F5828, F5833, F5837, F5846, F6001, F6096, F6104, F6114-6115, F6139, F6167-6168, F6187, F6234, F6253, H7118, H7123 and H7147-7148 were built up from spares in France.

DH6: Primarily built as trainers but several hundred of these recorded were transferred for coastal patrol and anti-submarine bombing. A9563-9762 (Grahame-White), B2601-3100, B8789-8790 and 8799-8800 built up from spares, B9031-9130, B9472 and B9992 built up from spares, C1951-2150 (Grahame-White), C3506 and C4281 built up from spares, C5126-5275 (Kingsbury), C5451-5750 (Harland & Wolff), C6501-6700 (Morgan & Co), C6801-6900 (Savages), C7201-7600 (Ransomes, Sims & Jeffries), C7601-7900 (Grahame White), C9336-9485 (Gloucestershire), C9994 built up from spares, D951-1000 (Grahame White), D8581-8780, F3346-3441.

DH9: A7559 prototype from converted DH4, B7581-7680 (Westland), B9331-9430 (Vulcan Motor & Engineering), C1151-1450 (G & J Weir), C2151-2230 (Berwick), C6051-6350, D451-950 (Cubitt) not all delivered, D1001-1500 (National Aircraft Factory No 2 built between 300 and 400 of numbers allotted), D1651-1750 (Mann, Egerton), D2776-2875 (Short Bros) special version with Fiat engines initially installed, D2876-3275, D5551-5850 (Waring & Gillow), D7201-7214 and D7217-7300 (Westland), D7301-7400 (Berwick) delivered as spares but several built up and given numbers in this range, E601-700 (Whitehead), E5435-5436, F1-142 (National Aircraft Factory No 1), F1101-1300 (Waring & Gillow), F1767-1866 (Westland) believed full deliveries not made due to Armistice, H5541-5890 (Alliance). In addition F5864, F6055, F6057, F6066, F6070, F6072-6073, F6112-6113, F6172, F6196, F6213 and H7176 were built up from spares in France.

DH9A: B7664 (Westland) DH9 prototype conversion, C6122 and C6350 further DH9 conversions, E701-1100 (Whitehead), E8407-8806, E9657-9756 (Mann, Egerton), E9857-9956 (Vulcan Motor & Engineering), F951-1100 and F1603-1652 (Westland), F2733-2882 (Berwick), F9515 being F963 rebuilt at Henlow, H1-200, H3396-3545 (Westland), H3546-3795 (Vulcan Motor & Engineering), H7107 rebuilt from salvage, J551-600 (Mann, Egerton), J6957-6962 (Westland), J6963-6968 (Handley Page), J7008-7017, J7018-7032 (Handley Page), J7033-7072 (Westland), J7073-7087 (Gloucestershire), J7088-7102 (Hawker Engineering), J7103-7127 assembled by RAF, Ascot Depot from spares, J7249-7258 (Gloucestershire), J7302-7309, J7310-7321 (Hawker Engineering), J7327-7346 (Westland), J7347-7356 (Gloucestershire), J7604-7615 (Hawker Engineering), J7700, J7787-7798, J7799-7819 (Westland), J7823-7834 (Short Bros), J7835-7854 (& J7867-7876) (Hawker), J7855-7866 (Westland), J7877-7883, J7884-7890 (Short Bros), J8096-8128 (Westland), J8129-8153, J8154-8171 (Short Bros), J8172-8189 (Parnall), J8190-8207 (Saunders), J8208-8225 (Blackburn), J8460-8482 (Westland), J8483-8494 (Parnall). **NB:** Aircraft from J7008 were mainly re-conditioned airframes and from J7787 mainly new airframes utilising existing spares. From J8460 all were fitted with dual control on production.

DH10 Amiens: C4283 fourth prototype numbered retrospectively, C8658-8660 first, second and third prototypes, E5437-5636 initial production of which the majority were completed, E6037-6136 (Birmingham Carriage) of which an initial few were built, E7837-7986 (Siddeley-Deasy) of which approximately the first 20 were built, E9057-9206 (Daimler) of which about 35 were built, F351-550 (National Aircraft Factory No 2) of which only the first few were completed, F1867-1882, F7147-7346 (Alliance) which were started but it is doubtful if any were built, F8421-8495 (Mann, Egerton) of which 20 or more were completed.

DH11 Oxford: H5891 prototype long distance day bomber.

DH14 Okapi: J1938-1940 ordered as long distance day bomber, with only first two completed as bomber prototypes.

DH15 Gazelle: J1937 basic DH9A with Atlantic engine installed.

DH27 Derby: J6894-6895 prototype single-engined heavy bombers.

DH72: J9184 three-engined night-bomber prototype.

Fairey IIIF: J9053-9077 Mk IVM, J9132-9156 Mk IV (GP) with wooden wings, J9157-9174 Mk IV (GP) with metal wings, J9637-9681 Mk IV and J9784-9831 Mk IV (GP), K1158-1170 Mk IV (GP), K1749-1778 Mk IVB. Many conversions to Gordon.

Fairey Fawn: J6907 Mk I, J6908-6909 Mk II, J6990-6991, J7182-7183 Mk I, J7184-7231 Mk II, J7768-7779 and J7978-7985 Mk III.

Fairey Fox: J7941 prototype, J7942-7958, J8423-8427, J9025-9028, J9515 and J9834 (see Chapter 15 for further details).

Fairey Gordon: J9154 prototype ex-Fairey IIIF Mk IV, K1729-1748 and K2683-2769 Mk I, K3986-4009 Mk II.

Fairey Hendon: K1695 prototype, K5085-5098 production.

Gloster Goring: J8674.

Gloster TC33: J9832 prototype bomber transport.

Handley Page 0/100: 1455-1466, 3115-3142, 3138 0/400 prototype.

Handley Page 0/400: B8802-8813 with Rolls-Royce Eagle engines (Royal Aircraft Factory), B9446-9451 with Sunbeam Cossack engines, C3381-3480 delayed order, C3487-3498 with Rolls-Royce Eagle engines (Royal Aircraft Factory), C9636-9785 completed with Rolls-Royce Eagle, Sunbeam Maori or Liberty engines as available, D4561-4660 for which Rolls-Royce Eagle or Liberty engines were specified (Metropolitan Wagon Company), D5401-5450 to which mainly Rolls-Royce Eagle engines were fitted (Birmingham Carriage Company), D8301-8350 (Handley Page, assisted by British Caudron and Harris Lebus), D9681-9730 with chiefly Rolls-Royce Eagle engines (Clayton & Shuttleworth), F301-320 with chiefly Rolls-Royce Eagle engines (Birmingham Carriage Company), F3748-3767 with Rolls-Royce Eagle or Liberty engines specified, F5349-5448 with Rolls-Royce Eagle or Liberty engines specified (National Aircraft Factory No 1), J2242-2291 with mainly Rolls-Royce Eagle engines (Birmingham Carriage Company), J6574-6576 replacements for F5414, F5417 and F5418, J6578 replacement for D8350.

Handley Page V/1500: B9463-9465 prototypes, E4304-4323 (prefabricated by Harland & Wolff and assembled by Handley Page), E8287-8306 (Beardmore), F7134-7143 (Alliance), J1935-1936 built up from spares, J6573 with Napier Lion engines was replacement for F7140.

Handley Page Chitral: Name change to Clive.

Handley Page Clive: J9126 Mk I experimental bomber transport of wooden construction converted to Mk III. J9948-9949 Mk II metal construction version.

Handley Page Handcross: J7498-7500 experimental day bombers.

Handley Page Hare: J8622 experimental day bomber/torpedo bomber.

Handley Page Heyford: J9130 prototype, K3489 non-standard first production, K3490-3502 Mk I, K3503 Mk I converted to Mk II and III, K4021 Mk I converted to Mk III, K4022-4043 Mk IA, K4863-4878 Mk II, K5180-5199 and K6857-6906 Mk III. (A note on each individual aircraft is given in Chapter 18.)

Handley Page Hinaidi: J7741 and J7745 converted from Hyderabads, J9031-9036 and J9298-9303 Mk I, J9478 prototype Mk II, K1063-1078 and K1909-1925 Mk II.

Handley Page Hyderabad: J6994 prototype, J7738-7752, J8317-8324, J8805-8815, J9293-9297.

Hawker Harrier: J8325 experimental two-seat day bomber/torpedo bomber of 1927.

Hawker Hart: J9052 prototype, J9933-9947, K1416-1447 and K2424-2473, K2966-3030 (Vickers at Weybridge), K3031-3054 (Armstrong Whitworth), K3808-3854 (Vickers at Weybridge); K3855-3872, K3875-3904, K3955-3972 and K4437-4495 (Armstrong Whitworth). (Harts built as trainers or communication aircraft are not included, but many of those built as day bombers, listed above, were subsequently converted to trainers.)

Hawker Hind: K2915 prototype, K4636-4655 K5368-5560, K6613-6856, L7174-7223. (Built as day bombers but many converted subsequently to trainers.)

Hawker Horsley: J7511 and J7721 prototypes, J7987-8026, Mks I and II according to wooden construction or composite wood and metal construction respectively, J8601-8620 Mk II, J8932 prototype all-metal version. Foregoing built as day bomber/torpedo bomber; all subsequent, not listed, built primarily as torpedo bombers.

Henri Farman: 188, 208, 274-275, 277-278, 283-284, 286, 294-295, 339, 341, 350-353, 412, 434-435, 440, 444-445, 455-456, 461, 467, 490, 502-513, 558-566, 653, 669, 680, 708, 720, 915 and 940 (Aircraft Manufacturing Company), 1321 (Grahame-White), 1368 and 1454 (Aircraft Manufacturing Company), 1518-1533, 1599 (South Coast Aviation), 1801-1806, 1813-1814, 1817-1818, 1821-1824, 2832, 2838 (Aircraft Manufacturing Company), 2844, 2851, 3150, 3617-3636, 3682, 3900-3919, 3998, 7746-7749, 7752-7755, 8238-8249, 9099, 9134-9153, A387-410. Up to this point aircraft used for operations or training, but all subsequent, not listed, were built solely for training.

Kennedy Giant: 2337 experimental prototype bomber.

Martinsyde Elephant: 4735 prototype, 7258-7307 and 7459-7508 G100 version, A3935-4004 and A6250-6299 G102 version.

Maurice Farman S11 Shorthorn: 342-345, 369-371, 379, 514-518, 540-545, 742, 1127, 1380-1387, 1839-1841, 1844, 1893, 2940-2959, 5004, 5008-5009, 5015, 5018-5019, 5027, 5030, 5036, 5054, 5059, 5071. (All subsequent acquisitions for training use only.)

Nieuport London: H1740-1741 experimental night bombers.

RE5: 26, 361, 380, 382, 631, 651, 659, 674, 677-678, 688, 737, 745, 2456-2459, 2461.

RE7: 2185-2234 (Coventry Ordnance Works), 2235-2236, 2237-2266 (Austin), 2287-2336 (Napier), 2348-2447 (Siddeley-Deasy).

Short Bomber: 3706 prototype, 9306-9340, 9356-9375 (Sunbeam), 9476-9495 (Mann, Egerton), 9771-9776 (Parnall), 9831-9836 (Phoenix Dynamo). Numbers transferred from RNAS and re-numbered in RFC, eg, A3932 ex-9833, A4005 ex-9325, A5153 ex-9484, A5154 ex-9483, A5155 ex-9319, A5157 ex-9316, A5158 ex-9480, A5159 ex-9481, A5170 ex-9478, A5171 ex-9772, A5173 ex-9485, A5179 ex-9482, A5180 ex-9477, A5181 ex-9488, A5182 ex-9476, A5203 ex-9315, A5214 ex-9320, A5488 built from RNAS spares, A5489 ex-9479, A5490 ex-9487, A6300 ex-9832.

Sopwith 1½ Strutter: 3686 two-seater prototype, designated A1, 9376-9425 two-seat, 9651-9652 single-seat, 9654 two-seat, 9655 single-seat, 9656 two-seat, 9657 single-seat, 9658-9659 two-seat, 9660-9661 single-seat, 9662-9663 two-seat, 9664 single-seat, 9665 two-seat, 9666 single-seat, 9667-9668 two-seat, 9669-9670 single-seat, 9671-9672 two-seat, 9673 single-seat, 9674 two-seat, 9675-9676 two-seat re-numbered A888 and

89 *Prototype Handley Page Heyford J9130 with 'dustbin' gun position fully lowered.*

90 *Prototype Handley Page Heyford J9130 with 'dustbin' gun position fully retracted.*

91 *Handley Page Heyford 'K' of No 10 Squadron. Note external bomb racks for 3 × 120 lb bombs; further outboard racks for 3 × 20 lb bombs or flares could be fitted.*

92 *Handley Page Heyford 'K' of No 7 Squadron, like the aircraft above, wearing the yellow trim of 'B' Flights.*

157

93 and 94 (*Upper*) *Hawker Hind of No 107 Squadron, and* (*lower*) *first production Fairey Hendon K5085 in Nivo (Ministry of Defence 8901B).*

95 *The effectiveness of Nivo is apparent from this aerial view of the Hendon Air Pageant 1932. At bottom left is the Heyford with the Boulton & Paul P32 experimental night bomber above it and a Fairey Hendon to the right.* **96** *The Heyford is shown again still bearing its Pageant Air Park Display No 12.*

97 *The slight sheen of Nivo can be seen in this view along the top fuselage surfaces.*

98 *An effective view of the Nivo-treated fabric stretched taut over the ribbing of the framework.*

99 *Prototype Hendon with open cockpits and two-bladed propellers. Fairey Gordons in background.*

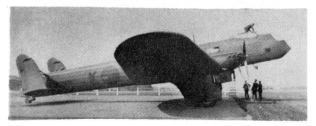

100 *Late service Hendon with revised cockpit cover—at the time this photo was taken the nose gun position cover had been removed. The black fuselage serials are just visible; aircraft is coded 'K'.*

A889, 9677 two-seat, 9678 and 9679 two-seat re-numbered A890 and
A896, 9680 two-seat, 9681 two-seat re-numbered A891, 9682-9699
two-seat, 9700 single-seat, 9701-9705 two-seat, 9706 single-seat, 9707-
9708 two-seat, 9709 single-seat, 9710 two-seat, 9711 single-seat, 9712-
9713 two-seat, 9714-9715 single-seat, 9716-9717 two-seat, 9718 single-
seat, 9719 two-seat, 9720 single-seat, 9721-9722 two-seat, 9723-9724
single-seat, 9725-9726 two-seat, 9727 single-seat, 9728 two-seat, 9729
single-seat, 9730-9731 two-seat, 9732-9733 single-seat, 9734-9735 two-
seat, 9736 single-seat, 9737 two-seat, 9738 single-seat, 9739-9740 two-
seat, 9741-9742 single-seat, 9743-9744 two-seat, 9745 single-seat, 9746
two-seat, 9747 single-seat, 9748-9750 two-seat, 9891-9897 two-seat, A377-
386 and A878-887 two-seat, A888-889 two-seat ex-9675-9676, A890 two-
seat ex-9678, A891 two-seat ex-9681, A892-895 two-seat, A896 two-seat
ex-9679, A897 two-seat, A954-1053 (Fairey Aviation), A1054-1153
(Vickers at Crayford) two-seat used mainly as fighters, A1511-1560
(Hooper) two-seat used mainly as fighters, A1902-1931 two-seat used
mainly as fighters, A2381-2430 (Ruston Proctor) two-seat used mainly
as fighters, A2431-2432 two-seat, A2983-2991 two-seat, A5238-5337
(Wells Aviation) two-seat but not all completed, A5950-6149 (Morgan)
two-seat but A6014-6015 were produced as single-seat bombers, A6901-
7000 (Hooper) two-seat but A6901, A6906, A6914, A6943, A6993 and
possibly others were produced as single-seat bombers and placed in
reserve, A8141-8340 (Ruston Proctor) produced in two- and single-seat
versions, A8744-8793 (Vickers at Crayford) two-seat mainly used as
fighters, N5080-5087 two-seat, N5088-5089 single-seat, N5090 two-seat,
N5091-5092 single-seat, N5093 two-seat, N5094-5095 single-seat passed
over to French, N5096 two-seat, N5097-5098 single-seat passed over to
French, N5099 two-seat, N5100-5101 single-seat passed over to French,
N5102 two-seat, N5103 single-seat, N5104 single-seat passed over to
French, N5105 two-seat, N5106-5107 single-seat, N5108 two-seat,
N5109-5110 single-seat, N5111 two-seat, N5112 single-seat, N5113
single-seat passed over to French, N5114 two-seat, N5115-5116 single-
seat passed over to French, N5117 two-seat, N5118 single-seat passed
over to French, N5119 single-seat converted to two-seat, N5120-5121
(Westland) single-seat, 5122-5123 (Westland) single-seat passed over to
French, 5124 (Westland) single-seat, 5125-5149 (Westland) single-seat
passed over to French, N5150-5169 (Westland) single-seat, N5170-5179
two-seat, N5200-5203 (Mann, Egerton) single-seat, N5204 (Mann,
Egerton) single-seat converted to two-seat, N5205-5212 (Mann, Egerton)
single-seat, N5213 (Mann, Egerton) single-seat converted to two-seat,
N5214-5219 (Mann, Egerton) single-seat, N5220-5234 (Mann, Egerton)
two-seat, N5235-5242 (Mann, Egerton) two-seat passed over to Belgians,
N5243-5249 (Mann, Egerton) two-seat, N5500-5501 single-seat, N5502
single-seat passed to French, N5503-5505 single-seat, N5506 single-seat
converted to two-seat, N5507 single-seat passed over to French, N5508-
5510 single-seat, N5511 single-seat passed over to French, N5512-5513
single-seat, N5514 single-seat passed over to French, N5515 single-seat
converted to two-seat, N5516-5522 single-seat, N5523 single-seat passed
to French, N5524-5526 single-seat, N5527 single-seat converted to two-
seat, N5528-5537 single-seat, N5600-5604 (Westland) single-seat, N5605-
5624 (Westland) two-seat, N5630-5654 (Mann, Egerton) two-seat.

BOMBING COLOURS

Sopwith B1: B1496 prototype believed ex-N50.

Sopwith Cobham: Experimental twin-engined bomber H671 Mk II, H672 Mk I, H673 not completed.

Sopwith Rhino: Experimental single-engined triplane bomber, X7 and X8.

Sunbeam Bomber: N515 became H4424 experimental bomber.

Tarrant Tabor: Four-engined experimental bomber F1765 crashed on first take-off, May 26 1919. F1766 not completed.

Vickers Valentia: Bomber transports detailed individually in Chapter 10 including conversions from Victorias.

Vickers Vanox: Originally called Vannock. J9131 prototype experimental night bomber variously modified.

Vickers Vernon: Bomber transports. J6864-6883 Mk I, J6884-6893 Mk II, J6976-6980 and J7133-7142 Mk II, J7539-7548 Mk III.

Vickers Victoria: Bomber transports detailed individually in Chapter 10 including conversions to Valentia.

Vickers Vimy: B9952-9954 (Vickers at Bexley) prototypes, F701-850 (Vickers at Crayford) of which only about first dozen were built, F2915-2944 (Royal Aircraft Factory) re-numbered in H651-670 batch, F3146-3195 (Morgan) of which majority were delivered, F8596-8645 (Vickers at Weybridge) of which majority were delivered, F9146-9295 (Vickers at Weybridge) of which 50 were delivered, F9569-9570 (Vickers at Bexley) to replace B9952 and B9954 burnt at an early stage of development, H651-670 (Royal Aircraft Factory) ex-F2915-2944 batch, H5065-5139 (Westland) of which 25 were built, H9963 (Vickers at Weybridge), J7238-7247 (Vickers at Weybridge) first post-war contract, J7440-7454 and J7701-7705 (Vickers at Weybridge).

Westland Yeovil: Experimental day bomber J7508-7509 Mk I of composite wood/metal construction and J7510 Mk II with all-metal airframe.

APPENDIX V: British bombing aircraft manufacturers, 1914-37

(List includes aircraft built for other purposes that were adapted for bombing.)

Aircraft firm and location	Types produced	Marking characteristics on products
The Aircraft Manufacturing Company Ltd, Hendon, London NW	DH3, DH4, DH6, DH9, DH10	Serial number normally marked on last two stripes of rudder instead of centrally as by other constructors
The Alliance Aeroplane Company Ltd, Cambridge Road, Hammersmith, London	DH9	Standard to period
Sir W. G. Armstrong Whitworth & Company Ltd, Gosforth, Newcastle-on-Tyne	BE2c	Standard to period
Sir W. G. Armstrong Whitworth Aircraft Ltd, Parkside, Coventry	Hawker Hart	Standard to period
The Austin Motor Company (1914) Ltd, Northfield, Birmingham	RE7	Standard to period
A. V. Roe & Company Ltd (Avro), Clifton Street, Miles Platting, Manchester	504, 504A, 504B, 504C, Pike, Manchester	Winged triangle insignia on engine cowlings and the words A V ROE & Co LTD MANCHESTER marked in small lettering on rear fuselage
A. V. Roe & Company Ltd (Avro), Newton Heath, Manchester	Aldershot, Ava, Antelope	Standard to period
Barclay, Curle & Company Ltd, Whiteinch, Glasgow	BE2e	Standard to period
Wm Beardmore & Company Ltd, Dalmuir, Dunbartonshire	Handley Page V/1500	Standard to period
F. W. Berwick & Company Ltd, Park Royal, London NW	DH4, DH9	Standard to period
The Birmingham Carriage Company, Birmingham	DH10, Handley Page 0/400	Standard to period

Aircraft firm and location	Types produced	Marking characteristics on products
The Blackburn Aeroplane & Motor Company Ltd, Olympia, Leeds	BE2c, Kangaroo	Trademark of propeller flanked by the letters B and A in a circular motif marked large on fuselage or fin
Boulton & Paul Ltd, Riverside, Norwich	Bourges Bugle, FE2b, Sidestrand	Standard to period
Boulton Paul Ltd, Norwich	Overstrand	Standard to period
The British and Colonial Aeroplane Company Ltd, Filton, Bristol	Braemar	Standard to period
The Bristol Aeroplane Company Ltd, Filton, Bristol	Berkeley	Standard to period
The British Caudron Company Ltd, Cricklewood, London, and Alloa, Scotland	BE2c, Caudron GIV, Handley Page 0/400	Standard to period
The Brush Electrical Engineering Company Ltd, Loughborough	Avro 504C	Standard to period
Clayton & Shuttleworth Ltd, Stamp End Works, Lincoln	Handley Page 0/400	Firm's trademark marked small on rear fuselage
The Coventry Ordnance Works Ltd, Coventry	BE12, RE7	Standard to period
Cubitt Ltd, Croydon, Surrey	DH9	Standard to period
de Havilland Aircraft Company Ltd, Stag Lane Aerodrome, Edgware, Middlesex	DH9A, DH27, DH72	Standard to period
The Daimler Company Ltd, Coventry	BE12, DH10	Standard to period
William Denny & Bros, Dumbarton	BE2c	Standard to period
The Eastbourne Aviation Company Ltd, Eastbourne	BE2c	Standard to period
The Fairey Aviation Company, Ltd, Hayes, Middlesex	Sopwith 1½ Strutter, Fawn, Fox, IIIF, Gordon	Constructor's serial number with 'F' prefix marked small adjacent to official serial number
The Fairey Aviation Company Ltd, Stockport, Cheshire	Hendon	Standard to period in this case Nivo finish

Aircraft firm and location	Types produced	Marking characteristics on products
Richard Garrett & Sons, Leiston, Suffolk	FE2b	Standard to period
Glendower Aircraft Company Ltd, Kew, Surrey	DH4	Standard to period
The Gloucestershire Aircraft Company Ltd, Cheltenham, Gloucester	DH6, DH9A	Standard to period
Gloster Aircraft Company Ltd, Hucclecote, Gloucester	Goring, TC33	Standard to period
The Grahame-White Aviation Company Ltd, Hendon, London	BE2c, DH6	Standard to period. Firm noted for particularly good finish to products
Handley Page Ltd, Cricklewood, London	0/100, 0/400, V/1500, DH9A	Serial number usually marked smaller than normal and at extreme rear of fuselage
Harland & Wolff Ltd, Belfast, Northern Ireland	DH6, Handley Page V/1500	Standard to period
H.G. Hawker Engineering Company Ltd, Kingston-on-Thames, Surrey	Horsley, Harrier, DH9A	Standard to period
Hawker Aircraft Ltd, Kingston-on-Thames, Surrey	Hart, Hind	Standard to period
Hewlett & Blondeau Ltd, Oak Road, Legrave, Luton	BE2c	Standard to period
Hooper & Company Ltd, Chelsea, London	Sopwith 1½ Strutter	Standard to period
The Kingsbury Aviation Company, Kingsbury, Surrey	DH6	Standard to period
Mann, Egerton & Company Ltd, Aircraft Works, Norwich	Sopwith 1½ Strutter, Short Bomber, DH9, DH9A, DH10	Firm's name and address stencilled on rear fuselage of products. See illustration in Chapter 4
Martinsyde Ltd, Brooklands, Byfleet, Surrey	BE2c, G100, G102 Elephant	Serials invariably marked on fin after mid-1915
The Metropolitan Wagon Company, Birmingham	Handley Page 0/400	Standard to period
Morgan & Company, Leighton Buzzard, Bedfordshire	Sopwith 1½ Strutter, DH6, Vickers Vimy	Standard to period

165

Aircraft firm and location	Types produced	Marking characteristics on products
Napier & Miller Ltd, Old Kilpatrick, Dumbarton, Scotland	BE2e	Standard to period
National Aircraft Factory No 1, Waddon, Surrey	DH9	Standard to period
National Aircraft Factory No 2, Heaton Chapel, near Stockport	DH9, DH10	Standard to period
The Nieuport & General Aircraft Company Ltd, Cricklewood, London NW	London	Unusual, white serials on night finish
Palladium Autocars Ltd, London	DH4	Standard to period
Parnall & Sons Ltd, Mivart Street, Eastville, Bristol	DH9A, Short Bomber	Standard to period
The Phoenix Dynamo Manufacturing Company Ltd, Bradford	Short Bomber	Marking at rear of fuselage 'PHOENIX BRADFORD' with letters bowed to form an ellipse
Ransome, Sims & Jeffries Ipswich, Suffolk	DH6, FE2b	Standard to period
Royal Aircraft Factory (Royal Aircraft Establishment from April 1918)	BE2 all versions, RE5, RE7, FE2 all versions, Handley Page 0/400	Often marked serial with an apostrophe between prefix letter and number
Ruston, Proctor & Company Ltd, Lincoln	Sopwith 1½ Strutter, BE2c/d/e	Standard to period
Savage & Company, Kings Lynn, Norfolk	DH6, Voisin	Standard to period
Short Bros, Rochester, Kent	Short Bomber, DH9, DH9A	Firm's name and address marked in various forms on fuselage together with constructor's number prefixed by 's'
The Siddeley-Deasy Motor Car Company Ltd, Park Side, Coventry	RE7	Standard to period

Aircraft firm and location	Types produced	Marking characteristics on products
The Sopwith Aviation Company Ltd, Canbury Park Road, Kingston-upon-Thames, Surrey	1½ Strutter, Cobham, Rhino	Firm's name and address marked on fin up to the time of introduction of camouflage. Serial number usually displayed in a white rectangle
The Standard Motor Company Ltd, Cash's Lane, Coventry	BE12	Union Jack trademark transfer marked on outboard wing struts
Alex Stephens & Company, Glasgow	FE2b	Standard to period
The Sunbeam Motor Car Company Ltd, Wolverhampton	Sunbeam Bomber	Single example N515 bore the Sunbeam number 171
W. G. Tarrant Ltd, Byfleet, Surrey	Tabor	Single example completed, unusual in that wing roundels were marked on the middle of the three wings due to this wing having the largest span
Vickers Ltd, Knightsbridge, London SW, with aircraft factories at Bexley, Crayford and Weybridge	BE2c, Sopwith 1½ Strutter, Vimy	Standard to period
Vulcan Motor and Engineering Company (1906) Ltd, Crossens, Southport, Lancashire	BE2c/d/e, DH4, DH9, DH9A	Standard to period
Waring & Gillow Ltd, Cambridge Road, Hammersmith, London	DH9	Standard to period
G & J Weir Ltd, Cathcart, Glasgow	BE2c, FE2b, DH9	Standard to period
Wells & Company Ltd, Elystan Road, Chelsea, London	Sopwith 1½ Strutter	Standard to period
The Westland Aircraft Works, Yeovil, Somerset	Sopwith 1½ Strutter, DH4, DH9, DH9A	Firm's circular trademark marked on rear fuselage of products
Wolseley Motors Ltd, Adderley Park, Birmingham	BE2c/e	Standard to period

APPENDIX VI: Chronology of British bomber markings—Official instructions, 1914-37

October 22 1914: Royal Aircraft Factory issued report on visibility of Union Jacks displayed on aircraft following experiments with BE2a No 201 on October 19.

October 26 1914: Royal Naval Air Service issued instructions that aircraft were to wear the Union Jack on underside of lower wing.

December 11 1914: Roundel form adopted by Royal Flying Corps for marking under wings.

December 17 1914: Red ring national marking adopted by Royal Naval Air Service.

May 16 1915: Rudder striping with blue leading from the rudder post, red trailing and white in between adopted for all British aircraft.

June 23 1915: Use of roundels extended to fuselage sides and upper-surface of top wings.

November 1 1915: Royal Naval Air Service discontinued using red ring national markings to be in line with Royal Flying Corps aircraft. Roundel standardised at 5:3:1 proportions of blue, white and red diameters respectively.

April 23 1916: Squadron markings adopted for aircraft on the Western Front applicable to BE2c squadrons which were used *inter alia* for bombing operations.

June 1 1916: Camouflage of khaki-green generally adopted for operational aircraft. Precise date not mandatory.

September 12 1916: White circle adopted as national marking of night flying aircraft, which were mainly bombers, but in practice it was rarely used.

July 26 1917: Squadron markings suggested by GHQ, RFC, included four DH4 squadrons, as effected August 26 1917.

August 18 1917: Orders issued on standardisation of aircraft markings on Western Front and the gradual obliteration of unauthorised embellishments.

August 26 1917: Squadron markings authorised, affecting bomber squadrons as follows:

No 18 Sqn White square aft of fuselage roundel;
No 25 Sqn White crescent aft of fuselage roundel;
No 55 Sqn White triangle aft of fuselage roundel;
No 57 Sqn White disc aft of fuselage roundel.

November 5 1917: Further squadron marking changes authorised, affecting DH4 bomber squadrons as follows:

No 27 Sqn White vertical bar aft of fuselage roundel;
No 49 Sqn White dumb-bell aft of fuselage roundel.

December 3 1917: Decision taken that the markings allotted to Nos 55 and 49 Sqns would continue to be used in DH9s replacing the DH4s for which the markings were originally issued.

Markings recommended for new squadrons with DH9s as follows:

No 98 Sqn White zig-zag behind fuselage roundel;
No 99 Sqn White 18-inch band around rear fuselage;
No 103 Sqn White sloping bars, one each side of fuselage roundel;
No 104 Sqn Three white vertical bars behind fuselage roundel.

It was further recommended that the FE2bs of Nos 58, 83, 100, 101 and 102 Sqns, being mainly concerned with night bombing, should have no unit markings.

December 23 1917: Further revision of markings of units on Western Front.

January 3 1918: Nivo first recommended as finish for night bombers, and red and blue roundel (without the white inner circle) also recommended; both were effected later in the year.

March 22 1918: All unit markings for bombers on Western Front obliterated as a security measure following the launching of the German offensive the day previous.

August 6 1918: Steps taken to change night roundel from white circle to a roundel without any white, ie, red disc with blue outer.

October 30 1918: Following weathering tests, a specification for printed roundels was drafted but did not come into effect due to the Armistice.

December 18 1924: Distinguishing flight colours officially promulgated as

    'A' Flights   Red
    'B' Flights   Yellow
    'C' Flights   Blue

March 17 1927: Air Ministry issued order for all aircraft to bear serial numbers under the wings in 30-inch characters, each 18 inches wide of strokes 4 inches thick, reading from opposite wings for port and starboard sides, as illustrated for Sidestrand in Chapter 14.

July 15 1930: RAF notified that the colours of rudder striping on aircraft was to be in the reverse order, ie, red leading from the rudder post with blue trailing. This change was to effect a distinction between French and British aircraft.

September 29 1930: Contractors were instructed to effect the rudder striping change on aircraft delivered from this date.

October 31 1930: Rudder striping changes had to be effected by this date.

August 1 1934: Rudder striping discontinued and roundels reduced in size so that they did not overlap into ailerons. Object overall was to remove over-painting on control surfaces.

February 1 1936: Grenade form approved as the standard outline frame for bomber squadron badges marked on aircraft.

August 1 1937: Camouflage introduced for all operational aircraft on production

APPENDIX VII: Orders of Battle

Bombing units of the RAF in November 1918

Bombing units with the British Expeditionary Force, France and Belgium

No 18 Sqn with 3 Flts of DH4s being replaced by DH9As at La Brayelles
No 25 Sqn with 3 Flts of DH4s at La Brayelles
No 27 Sqn with 3 Flts of DH9s at Villers-les-Cagnicourt
No 38 Sqn with 3 Flts of FE2b night bombers at Harlebeke
No 49 Sqn with 3 Flts of DH9s at Villers-les-Cagnicourt
No 57 Sqn with 3 Flts of DH4s at Bethencourt
No 58 Sqn with 3 Flts of Handley Page 0/400s at Provin
No 83 Sqn with 3 Flts of FE2b night bombers at Estrées-en-Chaussée
No 98 Sqn with 3 Flts of DH9s at Abscon
No 101 Sqn with 3 Flts of FE2b night bombers at Hancourt
No 102 Sqn with 3 Flts of FE2b night bombers at Bevillers
No 103 Sqn with 3 Flts of DH9s at Ronchin
No 107 Sqn with 3 Flts of DH9s at Moislains
No 108 Sqn with 3 Flts of DH9s at Bisseghem
No 148 Sqn with 3 Flts of FE2b night bombers at Erre
No 149 Sqn with 3 Flts of FE2b night bombers at St Marguerite
No 202 Sqn with 3 Flts of DH4s (Eagle) at Dunkirk
No 205 Sqn with 3 Flts of DH4s being replaced by DH9As at Moislains
No 206 Sqn with 3 Flts of DH9s at Linselles
No 207 Sqn with 3 Flts of Handley Page 0/400s at Estrées-en-Chaussée
No 211 Sqn with 3 Flts of DH9s at Iris Farm
No 214 Sqn with 3 Flts of Handley Page 0/400s at Chemy
No 217 Sqn with 3 Flts of DH4s (Eagle) at Dunkirk
No 218 Sqn with 3 Flts of DH9s at Reumont
'I' Flt, an Independent Flight of FE2bs at Erre

Bombing units of the Indepedent Force, France

No 55 Sqn with 3 Flts of DH4s at Azelot
No 97 Sqn with 3 Flts of Handley Page 0/400s at Xaffrevillers
No 99 Sqn with 3 Flts of DH9s at Azelot
No 100 Sqn with 3 Flts of Handley Page 0/400s at Xaffrevillers
No 104 Sqn with 3 Flts of DH9s at Azelot
No 110 Sqn with 3 Flts of DH9As at Bettoncourt
No 115 Sqn with 3 Flts of Handley Page 0/400s at Roville
No 215 Sqn with 3 Flts of Handley Page 0/400s at Xaffrevillers
No 216 Sqn with 3 Flts of Handley Page 0/400s at Roville

Bombing units in the Minor Theatres

No 30 Sqn with four DH4s included in establishment in Mesopotamia
No 31 Sqn with BE2c/es available for bombing on North-West Frontier of India
No 47 Sqn with four DH9s included in establishment in Salonika
No 114 Sqn with BE2c/es available for bombing in India
No 142 Sqn with 1 Flight of DH9s in Palestine
No 144 Sqn reforming with DH9s on Mudros
No 147 Sqn mobilising as bomber squadron in Egypt

No 221 Sqn with Nos 552, 553 and 554 Flts of DH9s in transit
No 223 Sqn with Nos 559, 560 and 561 Flts of DH9s in transit
No 224 Sqn with Nos 496, 497 and 498 Flts of DH4s at Otranto
No 226 Sqn with Nos 472, 473 and 474 Flts of DH9s on Mudros
No 227 Sqn awaiting Capronis at Taranto
No 269 Sqn with Nos 431 and 432 Flts of DH9s at Port Said
No 562 Flt, an independent flight with DH9s of 17th Wing at Malta

Bombing units of Home Establishment

No 116 Sqn mobilising with FE2bs and Handley Page 0/400s at Bicester
No 117 Sqn mobilising as bomber squadron in Ireland
No 118 Sqn mobilising with Handley Page 0/400s
No 121 Sqn mobilising with DH4/DH9s at Bracebridge
No 122 Sqn mobilising with DH4/DH9s at Upper Heyford
No 123 Sqn mobilising with DH4/DH9s at Upper Heyford
No 156 Sqn mobilising as day bomber squadron at Thetford
No 166 Sqn with 1 Flt of Handley Page V/1500s almost operational at Bircham Newton
No 167 Sqn forming with Handley Page V/1500s at Bircham Newton
No 212 Sqn with Nos 490 and 557 Flts of DH9s and No 558 Flt converting to DH9As at Yarmouth
No 219 Sqn with Nos 555 and 556 Flts of DH9s at Manston
No 223 Sqn with No 491 Flt of DH9s at Dover
No 236 Sqn with No 493 Flt of DH9s at Mullion
No 246 Sqn with No 495 Flt of Blackburn Kangaroos at Seaton Carew
No 250 Sqn with No 494 Flt of DH9s at Padstow
No 254 Sqn with No 492 Flt of DH9s at Prawle
No 273 Sqn with No 534 Flt of DH9s at Covehithe

NB: Maritime bomber squadrons have been included with the exception of DH6 units.

Bomber units in mid-1925

No 1 Group, HQ Kidbrooke
No 9 Sqn with 2 Flts of Vimys at Manston, Kent
No 207 Sqn with 3 Flts of DH9s at Eastchurch, Kent
Armament and Gunnery School with several Fawns and DH9As at Eastchurch, Kent

No 3 Group, HQ Spittlegate
No 7 Sqn with 2 Flts of Virginias at Bircham Newton, Norfolk
No 15 Sqn with 3 Flts of DH9As at Martlesham Heath
No 22 Sqn with 3 Flts of miscellaneous test aircraft at Martlesham Heath
No 39 Sqn with 3 Flts of DH9As at Spittlegate, Lincs
No 99 Sqn with 2 Flts of Aldershots at Bircham Newton, Norfolk
No 100 Sqn with 3 Flts of Fawns at Spittlegate, Lincs

No 7 Group, HQ Andover
No 11 Sqn with 3 Flts of Fawns at Netheravon, Wilts

No 12 Sqn with 3 Flts of Fawns at Andover, Hants
No 58 Sqn with 2 Flts of Virginias at Worthy Down, Hants

Middle East Command, HQ Cairo
No 47 Sqn with 3 Flts of DH9As at Helwan
No 216 Sqn with 2 Flts of Vimys at Heliopolis

Iraq Command, HQ Baghdad
No 8 Sqn with 3 Flts of DH9As at Hinaidi
No 30 Sqn with 3 Flts of DH9As at Hinaidi
No 45 Sqn with 2 Flts of Vernons at Hinaidi
No 55 Sqn with 3 Flts of DH9As at Hinaidi
No 70 Sqn with 2 Flts of Vernons at Hinaidi
No 84 Sqn with 3 Flts of DH9As at Shaibah

RAF India, HQ Delhi
No 27 Sqn with 3 Flts of DH9As at Risalpur
No 60 Sqn with 3 Flts of DH9As at Risalpur

Bomber units in mid-1930

Wessex Bombing Area, HQ Andover
No 7 Sqn with 2 Flts of Virginias at Worthy Down, Hants
No 9 Sqn with 2 Flts of Virginias at Manston, Kent
No 10 Sqn with 2 Flts of Hyderabads at Upper Heyford, Oxfordshire
No 12 Sqn with 3 Flts of Foxes at Andover, Hants
No 33 Sqn with 3 Flts of Harts at Eastchurch, Kent
No 35 Sqn with 3 Flts of Fairey IIIFs at Bircham Newton, Norfolk
No 58 Sqn with 2 Flts of Virginias at Worthy Down, Hants
No 99 Sqn with 2 Flts of Hinaidis at Upper Heyford, Oxfordshire
No 100 Sqn with 3 Flts of Horsleys at Bicester, Oxfordshire
No 101 Sqn with 2 Flts of Sidestrands at Andover, Hants
No 207 Sqn with 3 Flts of Fairey IIIFs at Bircham Newton, Norfolk

No 1 Air Defence Army (Special Reserve and Auxiliary Air Force), HQ London
No 501 Sqn with a Flt of DH9As at Filton, Nr Bristol
No 502 Sqn with 2 Flts of Hyderabads at Aldergrove, N Ireland
No 503 Sqn with a Flt of Hyderabads at Waddington, Lincolnshire
No 504 Sqn with a Flt of Horsleys at Hucknall, Nottinghamshire
No 600 Sqn with 3 Flts of Wapitis and Avro 504Ns at Hendon, London NW9
No 601 Sqn with 3 Flts of Wapitis and Avro 504Ns at Hendon, London NW9
No 602 Sqn with 3 Flts of Wapitis and Avro 504Ns at Renfrew, Scotland
No 603 Sqn with 3 Flts of Wapitis and Avro 504Ns at Turnhouse, Scotland
No 605 Sqn with 3 Flts of Wapitis and Avro 504Ns at Castle Bromwich, Nr Birmingham
(**NB:** Nos 604, 607 and 608 Bomber Squadrons were only equipped with Avro 504N trainers at this stage.)

RAF Middle East, HQ Cairo

No 45 Sqn with 3 Flts of Fairey IIIFs at Helwan
No 47 Sqn with 3 Flts of Fairey IIIFs at Khartoum
No 216 Sqn with 2 Flts of Victorias at Heliopolis

RAF Transjordan and Palestine HQ Amman

No 14 Sqn with 3 Flts of Fairey IIIFs at Amman

Iraq Command, HQ Hinaidi

No 30 Sqn with 3 Flts of Wapitis at Mosul
No 55 Sqn with 3 Flts of Wapitis at Hinaidi
No 70 Sqn with 2 Flts of Victorias at Hinaidi
No 84 Sqn with 3 Flts of Wapitis at Shaibah

RAF India, HQ Simla

No 11 Sqn with 3 Flts of Wapitis at Risalpur
No 27 Sqn with 3 Flts of Wapitis at Kohat
No 39 Sqn with 3 Flts of Wapitis at Risalpur
No 60 Sqn with 3 Flts of Wapitis at Kohat

Aden Command, HQ Steamer Point, Aden

No 8 Sqn with 3 Flts of Fairey IIIFs at Khormaksar

NB: Other units using bomber types in limited numbers were:
    Central Flying School, Wittering: DH9A
    No 2 Flying Training School, Digby: DH9A, Vimy
    No 4 Flying Training School, Abu Sueir: DH9A, Vimy
    Night Flying Flight, Biggin Hill: Horsley

Bomber units in mid-1935

Western Area, HQ Andover

No 7 Sqn with 2 Flts of Virginias at Worthy Down, Hampshire
No 9 Sqn with 2 Flts of Virginias at Boscombe Down, Wiltshire
No 10 Sqn with 2 Flts of Heyfords at Boscombe Down, Wiltshire
No 12 Sqn with 3 Flts of Harts at Andover, Hampshire
No 58 Sqn with 2 Flts of Virginias at Worthy Down, Hampshire
No 99 Sqn with 2 Flts of Heyfords at Mildenhall, Suffolk
No 142 Sqn with 3 Flts of Harts at Andover, Hampshire
No 500 Sqn with 2 Flts of Virginias at Manston, Kent
No 502 Sqn with 2 Flts of Virginias at Aldergrove, N Ireland
No 503 Sqn with 2 Flts of Hinaidis at Waddington, Lincolnshire

Central Area, HQ Abingdon

No 15 Sqn with 3 Flts of Harts at Abingdon, Berkshire
No 18 Sqn with 3 Flts of Harts at Upper Heyford, Oxfordshire
No 33 Sqn with 3 Flts of Harts at Upper Heyford, Oxfordshire
No 35 Sqn with 3 Flts of Gordons at Bircham Newton, Norfolk
No 40 Sqn with 3 Flts of Gordons at Abingdon, Berkshire
No 57 Sqn with 3 Flts of Harts at Upper Heyford, Oxfordshire

No 101 Sqn with 2 Flts of Sidestrands at Bicester, Oxfordshire
No 207 Sqn with 3 Flts of Gordons at Bircham Newton, Norfolk
No 501 Sqn with 3 Flts of Wallaces at Filton, Nr Bristol
No 504 Sqn with 3 Flts of Wallaces at Hucknall, Nottinghamshire

No 1 Air Defence Group, HQ London
No 602 Sqn with 3 Flts of Harts at Abbotsinch, Scotland
No 603 Sqn with 3 Flts of Harts at Turnhouse, Scotland
No 605 Sqn with 3 Flts of Harts at Castle Bromwich, Nr Birmingham
No 607 Sqn with 3 Flts of Wapitis at Usworth, Co Durham
No 608 Sqn with 3 Flts of Wapitis at Thornaby, Yorkshire

RAF Middle East, HQ Cairo
No 45 Sqn with 3 Flts of Fairey IIIF(GP)s at Helwan
No 47 Sqn with 3 Flts of Gordons at Khartoum
No 216 Sqn with 3 Flts of Victorias at Heliopolis

Palestine and Transjordan Command, HQ Jerusalem
No 6 Sqn with 2 Flts of Gordons at Ismailia and 1 Flt at Ramleh
No 14 Sqn with 3 Flts of Gordons at Amman, Transjordan

British Forces Iraq, HQ Hinaidi
No 30 Sqn with 3 Flts of Wapitis at Mosul
No 55 Sqn with 3 Flts of Wapitis at Hinaidi
No 70 Sqn with 3 Flts of Victorias at Hinaidi
No 85 Sqn with 3 Flts of Vincents at Shaibah

RAF India, HQ Simla
No 11 Sqn with 3 Flts of Harts at Risalpur
No 27 Sqn with 3 Flts of Wapitis at Kohat
No 39 Sqn with 3 Flts of Harts at Risalpur
No 60 Sqn with 3 Flts of Wapitis at Kohat

Aden Command, HQ Steamer Point, Aden
No 8 Sqn with 3 Flts of Vincents at Khormaksar

Anti-Aircraft Co-operation Flight, Biggin Hill: Wallace
Communication Flight Iraq, Hinaidi: Wapiti
Bomber Transport Flight India, Lahore: Victoria VI and Valentia

NB: In addition, No 28 Squadron had Wapitis, but was classed as an Army Co-operation squadron, and Nos 600 and 601 Squadrons had Harts and No 604 Squadron Wapitis, but these were in the process of changing their role to fighter squadrons and were officially classed as such.

APPENDIX VIII: Presentation bomber aircraft inscriptions

DONORS OF AIRCRAFT, as described in Chapter 1, had two things in mind when giving money for the purchase of aircraft in the national interest, which were that they would be either fighters or bombers. The importance of reconnaissance and artillery ranging was lost upon the public at large—and, come to that, in some military circles too. The numbers of BE2cs presented were much larger than that of any other type and this no doubt was conditioned by its early use as a bomber.

Serial number	Type	Presentation inscription marked on aircraft	Remarks concerning service
1748	BE2c	LIVERPOOL	Served in No 6 Sqn Flew 139 hours before being scrapped, 1.8.15
2126	BE2c	LIVERPOOL	Replacement for 1748. Flown to France on 23.1.16 to No 6 Sqn
2127	BE2c	HONG KONG	Flown to France, 23.1.16. Served in No 6 and 8 Sqns
2361	RE7	THE AKYAB Overseas Club No 33	Served in No 19 Sqn Crashed April 1916
2480	BE2c	PUNJAB 35 MARIANA	Served in No 15 Sqn
2572	BE2c	JOHANNESBURG No 1	Flown to France, 15.1.16. Served in No 15 Sqn
2578	BE2c	RHODESIA No 3	Flown to France, 23.1.16. Modified for long range work. Served in No 15 Sqn
2679	BE2c	HAWKES BAY NEW ZEALAND	Flown to France, 18.10.15. Served in No 6 Sqn
6341	FE2b	ZANZIBAR I	Served in No 25 Sqn
6365	FE2b	MAURITIUS II	Served in No 22 Sqn Lost 11.7.16, pilot wounded and captured
6944	FE2b	NEWFOUNDLAND IV	Served in No 11 Sqn Crashed by hitting railway signal, 18.6.16
9383	Sopwith 1½ Strutter	BRITONS IN JAPAN No 1	Served in No 5 Wing
9395	Sopwith 1½ Strutter	Tiensin Britons No 1	Bombed Bruges harbour on 3.2.17 (early hours) and same target on 7.2.17

Serial number	Type	Presentation inscription marked on aircraft	Remarks concerning service
9401	Sopwith 1½ Strutter	POVERTY BAY NEW ZEALAND	Served in No 3 Wing. Had reported tendency to nose-dive on turns!
9405	Sopwith 1½ Strutter	Britons in Egypt No 1	Served in No 5 Wing at Dunkirk
9423	Sopwith 1½ Strutter	PEKING BRITONS No 1	Served in No 5 Wing. Returned to UK and survived the war
A3055	BE2e	THE ANZAC	Served in No 9 Sqn
A3065	BE2e	Presented by His Highness the Maharajah of Bikanir No 2	Served in Middle East
A3071	BE2e	ALEXANDRIA (EGYPT) BRITONS No 1	No details known
A5478	FE2b	GOLD COAST 10	Served in No 100 Sqn
A6286	Martinsyde Elephant	RHODESIA III	Replacement for former Rhodesia III
A6360	FE2d	AUSTRALIA No 10, NSW No 9	Served in No 57 Sqn
A6516	FE2d	THE TWEED	
		Presented by the Colony of Mauritius No 13	Served in No 20 Sqn
A7483	DH4	AUSTRALIA No 5, NSW No 4 PREST WHITE FAMILY	Served in No 18 Sqn
A7864	DH4	FELIXSTOWE	RAF3A engine fitted

Manufacturers markings on Short bombers

SHORT BROS.
AERONAUTICAL ENGINEERS
ROCHESTER, ENGLAND

Short Bros

THE SUNBEAM MOTOR CAR Co. LTD.

WOLVERHAMPTON

Sunbeam

PARNALL & SONS
AIRCRAFT
CONSTRUCTORS
BRISTOL ENGLAND

Parnall

MANN, EGERTON & Co L™
AIRCRAFT WORKS,
NORWICH,
ENGLAND.

Mann, Egerton

PHOENIX
BRADFORD

Phoenix

Characteristic manufacturers markings

THE
SOPWITH
AVIATION Company Ltd
KINGSTON ON THAMES

Sopwith 1 1/2 Strutter, 1916,
fin marking

AVRO

Avro 504, 1914–15
Engine cowling marking

A·W

Armstrong Whitworth, 1915–19
Engine cowling embossing

Nitro-dope symbols on fabric

(black)
Britannia

(red)
Cellon

(blue)
British Emaillite

Standard serial characters

ABCDEFHJKLNS
1234567890